M000296726

A Basic
Introduction to
Missions and Missiology

Glenn Rogers

Published by
Mission and Ministry Resources

ISBN: 0977439623
13 digit ISBN: 978-0-9774396-2-1

Book formatting and cover design by: Beth E. Miller

Visit our Website at:

www.missionandministryresources.net

Table of Contents

List of Figures

Introduction

Missiology is a multidisciplinary discipline. What does that mean? Theology is a specific discipline. It is an area of study where a student can focus his or her attention, becoming proficient in that discipline. Anthropology is also a discipline. So is History, Psychology and Philosophy. Each of them is an area of academic concentration. Missiology is also a specialized field of study. But it is a combination of at least three specific fields of study, or disciplines: theology, anthropology, and ecclesiology (specifically, church and mission history). Missiology, therefore, as an academic specialty or discipline, is *multidisciplinary*. The student of missions must be prepared to spend the time and exert the energy necessary to become proficient in more than one area of study.

This book is designed to give the student of missions: 1) an overview of the study of missiology and the different ways one can serve as a missionary, 2) some guidance in preparing for missionary field work, and 3) a glimpse of life as a missionary. It is a basic introduction, an overview. None of the topics are treated exhaustively. My purpose is to acquaint you with the broadly diverse field of missions studies, providing a foundation and framework for further studies. By giving readers a birds-eye-view of the whole field of study, I hope to assist them in seeing the significance and necessity of a broad base of foundational studies, as well as areas of specialty in which they may choose to narrow their focus for future concentration.

Part 1 begins with *Mission Concepts*, discussing God's purpose in creation and his desires for humanity, his activity in human history, and how he has invited his people to participate with him in accomplishing his mission in the world. This section also defines terms and explores concepts so students new to missions studies can become familiar with the vocabulary of the discipline.

Part 2, *Mission Training*, discusses the three-part division of mission studies: Word, World, and Church, a phraseology first coined by missiologist Dudley Woodberry. That three-part division consists of biblical studies (Word), anthropological studies (world), ecclesiastical studies related to church and mission history. I will also discuss areas of concentration within the field of missiology, identifying and briefly explaining what is entailed in each.

Part 3, *Mission Work*, highlights some of the ways mission can be accomplished, that is, ways individuals can serve as missionaries in foreign or local mission outreach efforts. This section also discusses preparation for going into the field, living as a missionary in a cross-cultural setting, and being part of the larger missionary/missiological community. There is also a section that includes a list of books for further study. Each entry will include the necessary bibliographic information, a brief overview of the book and why it is important for further missiological study.

Part I

Mission Concepts

Why did God create humans in his image? What did he have in mind when he selected Abraham and created the nation of Israel? Why has he been so active in human history over the centuries? Why communicate with humans and see to it that a record of that communication and his interaction in human history was preserved and made available to human beings? Why did he become human, coming to earth in the person of Jesus, offering himself as a sacrifice of atonement? Why has he asked people of faith to tell the story of Jesus to every ethnic group on the planet? These are foundational questions that must be answered at the initial stages of missiological inquiry. In this first section, I will discuss these questions and concepts, focusing on God's purpose in creation, his mission in the world and how believers participate with him in that mission.

Equally important in the initial stages of missiological inquiry is a firm grasp of the specialized vocabulary that has developed in the discipline. Since missiology is multidisciplinary, heavily influenced by anthropology and theology, a number of technical terms have developed that students must understand if they are to interact effectively with the material, professors and other missiological students. Therefore, in this first section, I will also take time to discuss some basic missiological terminology. It is not my intention to create an exhaustive glossary of missiological vocabulary, but only to introduce some basic terminology. Other important words and ideas will be defined and discussed in appropriate sections.

Chapter 1

God's Mission—Our Mission

God's Mission

To understand what God wants today, what he plans to accomplish in his world, we must think about what he wanted when he created humans *in his image*. He has not specifically explained why he created humans, or why he created them in his image. We must understand his creative intent by examining his creative action, and his response to the actions of people he created in his likeness.

Relationship

What does it mean to be created in God's image and likeness? The Hebrew words for image (*tselem*) and likeness (*demewth*) do not provide much help in answering the question. Basically, both words refer to resemblance. God created humans so that we resemble him in some way. But in what way? *Tselem* and *demewth* usually refer to physical resemblance (Wenham 1987:29-31, Matthews 1996:165-172). Physical resemblance, however, is not the point. God is not a physical being. Jesus said that God is a spirit (Jn. 4:24). God does not look like any aspect of his physical creation—including the physical form of his human children. Recognizing this, however, does not mean that it is appropriate to simply toss out the fact that we are physical creatures and discuss the image of God as if it applied only to spiritual concerns (Kidner 1967:50-51).

John Goldingay suggests that God created us in his image for *relational* reasons. We exist in relation to him, to each other, and to the world around us. He wanted us to take care of the world he created, so he made us like him, giving us the abilities and authority we would need to do the job—ability and authority that resemble his own. He also made us relational beings, able to relate to each other and to him because we are like him (Goldingay 1998:6-9). Ray Anderson makes a similar observation, including our physical nature as part of what it means to be created in the image of God. It is in or by means of our physical bodies that we relate to other people, and in the sexual relationship that we cooperate with God to create life (1982:86). The image of God is not limited to spiritual, intellectual or emotional likeness, but includes our physical bodies, which are integral to our living in relationship with him and others.

Von Rad points out that the use of the Hebrew *bara* (create) occurs three times in one verse (Gen. 1:27) to highlight the significance of God's creativity as it relates to humans (1961:57). Brueggemann observes that:

It is important that of all the creatures of God's eight creative acts, God speaks directly only to human creatures. The others have no speech directed toward them at all. By contrast, in 1:28, God speaks to the human creatures, and in verse 29, he twice addresses them directly, "you." This creature has a different, intimate relation with the creator. This is the speech-creature *par excellence*. This is the one to whom God has made a particularly intense commitment (by speaking) and to whom marvelous freedom has been granted (in responding), (1982:31)

Porter agrees, suggesting that we can communicate with

God and respond to him because we are like him (1993:140).

In Genesis 1, the highlight of God's activity is clearly his creation of humans in his image. He created people in his image so they could care for the world he created. But on a more fundamental level, God created people in his image so he and they could enjoy a mutually satisfying relationship with each other. That this was his basic creative purpose can be seen in the symbolism of the creation narrative of Genesis 2.

The creation narrative of Genesis 2 is probably the older of the two Hebrew oral traditions regarding creation (Willis 1979:115). In this narrative, God is the creative force behind everything that exists, but the focus is not on the order in which God created the material world, but on humans as the central focus of his creative energy. In Genesis 1, the creation of male and female is represented briefly as a single creative event. In Genesis 2, the creation of male occurs first. Adam is created first, and for a while is alone. But God recognizes that being a one-of-a-kind being is not a good thing. God wanted Adam to understand his uniqueness, so all the animals were brought before Adam to see if he could identify one that could serve as his companion. None of the animals measured up to Adam. None of them were suitable to be Adam's companion. Why not? Because none of them were like him. God wanted Adam to understand what he (God) understood: you can't have a meaningful, mutually satisfying relationship with a creature that is not like you. Once Adam understood this, God created Eve. Eve was like Adam. She was a human being created in God's image. She was just the same as Adam. She was a female version, but aside from that she was the same as Adam. Hamilton observes that the Hebrew of Gen. 2:18 represents Eve as one who *corresponds* to Adam (1990:175). She is his female counterpart.

❀ *I suggest that this creation narrative focusing on Adam's need for someone like himself with whom he can enjoy a relationship is symbolically representative of God's desire for others like himself with whom he can enjoy a relationship.* Since meaningful relationship requires likeness or sameness, God created people in his image, in his likeness.

B. W. Anderson has observed:

> Man is made to have fellowship with God. He is the only creature who can answer God, either in defiance or in trust. Although all of God's creatures are summoned to praise him, man is the only creature in whom praise can become articulate. His life is made for conversation with God, for a dialogue in an I-and-thou relation (1962:729-730).

Along those same lines, Newbigin has said:

> I believe that the Christian view of God's purpose for the human family. . . arises from a distinct belief about what human nature is. From its first page to its last, the Bible is informed by a vision of human nature for which neither freedom nor equality is fundamental; what is fundamental is relatedness. Man—male and female—is made for God in such a way that being in the image of God involves being bound together in this most profound of all mutual relations (1986:118).

Reconciliation

Chapters 1 and 2 of Genesis help us understand what God wants. He wants a relationship with people. That is why he created people in his image. But chapters 1 and 2 tell us only part of the story. Chapter 3 adds another significant element. It sets the stage for our understanding of how important God's relationship with his human children is to him.

We know the story. The serpent, representative of humankind's antagonist (Matthews 1996:232), comes to Eve asking questions and making statements designed to create doubt in her mind as to God's motive for the restriction he placed on the human couple. The serpent lied to her. It was not a big lie. It was a misrepresentation of the truth—but not so much of a misrepresentation that it was unbelievable. God had said that if they ate of the fruit they would die. Satan said they would not. God was talking about the spiritual consequences. Satan was talking about the physical. He was right in that they did not die physically. But that is not what God had meant. Satan misrepresented the truth. He also suggested that God's motive was self-serving, focused on keeping his human children subordinate rather than allowing them to become equals. Satan's approach was so believable that Eve believed what he said and disobeyed God. Adam, too, for some reason we cannot be sure about, went along with Eve, disobeying God, severing the intimate relationship he had with his Father.

Why did their disobedience destroy the relationship they had with God? Because they believed lies about God. They doubted his love and truthfulness. Their disobedience was rooted in behavior contrary to God's nature. They allowed sin to become a reality in their lives, diminishing or tarnishing the image of God in themselves. God is perfect. They had been created in his image. They, too, had been perfect. There was nothing ungodly about them—until they allowed Satan to influence them so that behavior contrary to the holiness and glory of God stained and soiled them, making them less than they had been before. The perfect and complete harmony they had enjoyed with God was broken because that which cannot exist in harmony with God became a factor in their lives. They suffered the spiritual death God had warned them about.

How did God react? This is the most important part of the story. God could have rejected them utterly and completely forever. They had believed a lie about him and had disobeyed, breaking his heart in the process. God would have been completely justified if he had turned away from them forever. But instead, he came looking for them.

Verse eight refers to the *sound* of God walking in the garden. The Hebrew *qol,* often means voice, but Von Rad points out that here, as in 2 Sam. 5:24, it refers to "the rustle of God's step," (1961:91). When Adam and Eve heard the sound they recognized it. It was God. Hamilton notes that the Hebrew verb which describes God's movement (*mithallek*) indicates habitual action (1990:192). Obviously God had come to visit them before—and not just once. He had made a habit of it. Wenham suggests that a "daily chat between the almighty and his creatures was customary," (1987:76). Mathews refers to God's visit as an anthropomorphism (1996:239). I believe the term theophany would be more accurate. Evidently God would take a human form and come each day to the garden to interact with his human children—to talk with them, or even to run and play with them. Why? To enjoy the relationship for which he had created them. How long had this been going on before the serpent appeared and tempted Eve? It is impossible to tell. Perhaps years, centuries, or even millennia (Rogers 2002:71).

What happened when God came to visit his human children? Adam and Eve hid from their Father. What did God do? He called out to them. *"Adam, where are you?"* Why? He could have simply turned and walked away. He could have withdrawn his presence from the world, abandoning the humans who had believed a lie about him and broken faith with him. But he did not. Why not? Because he had created people to enjoy a relationship with them. Because even though they had hurt him, he still loved them and still wanted the relationship he had envisioned before sin spoiled the companionship they had enjoyed. You don't walk away from people you love.

Then we come to Genesis 3:16, a passage scholars feel is the first statement that looks forward to the death of Jesus, an event that would make reconciliation between a holy God and sinful humans possible. It looks forward to a time when God would take it upon himself to solve the problem humans caused but could not resolve. It looks forward to a time when God himself would become a human being, living among us, showing us what he is like and how he wants us to live in this world. It looks forward to the sacrifice for the sins of all people, so all people could be reconciled to God through faith. Nearly everything God did in human history between his visit to the garden that day and his coming in the person of Jesus was to get things ready for his appearance as a human being and his sacrifice of atonement for sin.

God's primary purpose in all his interaction in human history was rooted in his desire for a relationship with all people. That is what God wants. His mission in this world, the *missio Dei*, is for all people to be reconciled to him, to be brought back into an intimate, mutually satisfying relationship with him. And he wants us to help him accomplish that mission.

Our Mission. . . Modeled After Jesus' Own Mission

Jesus came to seek and save the lost (Lk. 19:10). He came not to be served, but to serve and to offer himself as a ransom for those captive to Satan (Mt. 20:28). When Jesus had accomplished his purpose, making it possible for all people to be reconciled to God, he commissioned his followers to spread the news that a renewed relationship with God was now possible. God's original creative goal of a mutually satisfying

9

relationship with all people was possible because of what he had accomplished through the substitutionary death of Jesus. Jesus' followers, therefore, were to go to all groups of people (*panta ta ethna*), telling them the story of God, humanity, sin and salvation through Jesus so all people could become followers of Jesus, enjoying the reconciliation his death made possible (Mt. 28:18-20).

God has called his people to participate with him in accomplishing his mission in the world—the reconciliation of all lost people. How do we do that? Since Jesus was God living as a human being, accomplishing the Father's plan for making reconciliation possible, the way Jesus went about accomplishing God's mission in the world is a good place for us to begin investigating how we should go about working together with God to accomplish his mission in the world.

As noted above, Jesus came to save the lost, that is, to make it possible for God's human children, estranged from their Father because of sin, to be re-united with him. That was God's mission when he came in the person of Jesus. Reconciliation was what he meant to accomplish. To make a relationship with him possible and desirable, God had to let us see him in action, making himself known to us so we would want to get to know him better. Related to the basic mission of reconciliation was the need for revelation—God's desire to introduce himself and make himself available to us in a concrete way. This is John's point in the prolog of his gospel. The incarnation was *God's self-portrait* (Lyons 1994), his making himself fully available to his human children so they could understand him, get to know him, and, hopefully, allow him to solve the relationship problem they had created.

Out of those two basic goals, revelation and reconciliation, came a number of specific mission and ministry activities designed to accomplish those basic goals. What were they? How did Jesus reveal God to us? Through: 1) godly living, 2)

10

godly teaching, and 3) godly concern for others. How did Jesus make reconciliation possible for all people? By his personal sacrifice. If Jesus accomplished his mission and ministry in these ways, we should follow his example, using those same methods to accomplish our mission and ministry.

Godly Living

The word *godly* or *godliness* is from the Greek word *eusebeia*, meaning a piety or holiness characteristic of one who prefers to be close to God, one who wants to please God. A godly person is inclined toward God to the degree that he or she is God-serving rather than self-serving. His or her focus in life is living the way God would have him or her to live rather than living according to personal dictates and desires. Paul reminded Titus about the importance of godly living:

> *For the grace of God that brings salvation has appeared to all men. It teaches us to say "No" to ungodliness and worldly passions, and to live self-controlled, upright and godly lives in this present age, while we wait for the blessed hope-the glorious appearing of our great God and Savior, Jesus Christ, who gave himself for us to redeem us from all wickedness and to purify for himself a people that are his very own, eager to do what is good* (Titus 2:11-14).

In his letter to the Romans Paul expressed the same idea in slightly different words.

> *Therefore, I urge you, brothers, in view of God's mercy, to offer your bodies as living sacrifices, holy and pleasing to God-this is your spiritual act of worship. Do not conform any longer to the pattern of*

this world, but be transformed by the renewing of your mind. Then you will be able to test and approve what God's will is-his good, pleasing and perfect will (Rom. 12:1-2).

When we are inclined toward God, we live as he would have us live, allowing his image to shine through in our daily lives for all to see. We reveal God to others by the way we live just as Jesus revealed God by the way he lived. We do not reveal God to others as well as Jesus did because as much as we try to avoid sinning, we remain sinful people. In spite of our sinfulness, however, God makes himself visible to the world through his people. Thus, our mission and ministry is *incarnational* (Van Rheenen 1996:72-73), revealing God to the world. God is present in his world through his people.

Godly Teaching

We also reveal God to the world by the things we teach. Like godly living, godly teaching is teaching that is "inclined toward"—inclined toward God's word and what he communicates to us in it. Godly teaching is rooted in the message of Scripture, not in culturally impacted human opinion or systematic statements of theology and doctrine. It is a *re-communication* of the message God has communicated to us in the Scriptures: his desire for a relationship with all people. That *metatheme* underlies and unifies the whole of God's communication, giving deeper meaning to all the other themes and motifs we find in Scripture—kingdom, covenant, etc. (Rogers 2002). When our teaching about God reflects his desire for a relationship with each person, we are revealing one of the most significant factors humans need to know about God. We are revealing his purpose in creation, the reason for his involvement in human history, his reason for becoming a human being, offering himself as a sacrifice of atonement, and his reason for sending believers into the world with his message of reconciliation.

Paul's inclination toward God was so complete that not only was his teaching rooted in the message of reconciliation, his personal identity as well was defined by the message he had been asked to re-communicate. He thought of himself as an ambassador of Christ.

> *So from now on we regard no one from a worldly point of view. Though we once regarded Christ in this way, we do so no longer. Therefore, if anyone is in Christ, he is a new creation; the old has gone, the new has come! All this is from God, who reconciled us to himself through Christ and gave us the ministry of reconciliation: that God was reconciling the world to himself in Christ, not counting men's sins against them. And he has committed to us the message of reconciliation. We are therefore Christ's ambassadors, as though God were making his appeal through us. We implore you on Christ's behalf: Be reconciled to God. God made him who had no sin to be sin for us, so that in him we might become the righteousness of God (2 Cor. 5:16-21).*

Godly teaching does not just reveal facts or information about God, it reveals God's heart, God's love, God's desire to have his estranged children come back to him. For godly teaching to be effective, it must be combined with godly living. The combination of the two provide people with the most complete picture of God and the Good News of the Gospel.

Godly Concern For Others

When our concern for others reflects the same concern God has for them, we are exhibiting a godly concern for others. Our inclination toward God is strong enough that his concern for others shines through in our own lives. In what ways is God concerned for others? The metatheme of God's communication to us is his desire for a relationship with all people. His primary concern is for their spiritual needs. But God is also concerned about the quality of people's lives. God provided for Adam and Eve's physical needs when they lived in the garden. He created the world with everything humans need to survive available to them. He provided for Israel's needs as they wandered in the desert. During Jesus' ministry he taught that we must be concerned about the physical needs of others. We must love others as much as we love ourselves, even meeting the physical needs of those we may count among our enemies. We are to be especially mindful of the physical needs of those more vulnerable than ourselves: widows and orphans, the sick and the oppressed. A hungry person must be fed. A thirsty person must be given a drink. A cold person must be given something with which to keep warm.

Jesus taught, and by his life, modeled godly concern for others. His concern was not only demonstrated in preaching the good news of the kingdom, but in healing the sick, feeding the hungry and displays of compassion for those spiritually, physically and emotionally oppressed. God's concern for others was revealed in Jesus' concern for others. Our concern for others will also reveal God's concern for others.

Personal Sacrifice

Jesus' inclination toward God is demonstrated most fully in his willingness to make the ultimate personal sacrifice.

14

Jesus said, *"The reason my Father loves me is that I lay down my life-only to take it up again. No one takes it from me, but I lay it down of my own accord. I have authority to lay it down and authority to take it up again. This command I received from my Father"* (Jn. 10:17-18).

As a human being, Jesus had the same instinctive drives for survival and life that we have. He did not like pain. He did not have a death wish. He did not want to be betrayed, tortured and executed. But he had a clear vision of what needed to be done. He understood that eternity hung in the balance for all of humankind. He understood the Father's desire for a relationship with the people he had created in his own image. And he understood that unless he acted on behalf of all people, all people would have only condemnation to look forward to on judgment day. He was willing to sacrifice his physical life in exchange for the hope of salvation for all people. It was his life against our souls. Himself or us. He chose us.

Jesus made reconciliation for all people possible by his personal sacrifice. We are not confronted with a spiritual dilemma that is as cosmic in scope as was Jesus. But we are confronted with the opportunity to make our own personal sacrifice for the good of others. In contemplating the depth of our own personal sacrifice, Paul suggests that we follow Jesus' example.

> *Your attitude should be the same as that of Christ Jesus: Who, being in very nature God, did not consider equality with God something to be grasped, but made himself nothing, taking the very nature of a servant, being made in human likeness. And being found in appearance as a man, he humbled himself and became obedient to death- even death on a cross!* (Phil 2:5-8).

15

The more we are inclined toward God, the more willing we will be to make the personal sacrifices necessary to participate with him in his mission in the world, his mission of revelation and reconciliation.

Summary

What does God want? God wants a relationship with all people. He created us in his image so both he and we could enjoy a mutually satisfying relationship with each other. When sin became a reality of human existence, God did not turn away. Rather, he reached out to his estranged children, offering them mercy and the possibility of reconciliation through the substitutionary death of Jesus. Re-establishing a relationship with each person became God's mission. Those who have re-established a relationship with him are invited to participate with him in the reconciliation of others. Following Jesus' mission and ministry model, we carry out our mission of making God known to a lost world (revelation) and helping others re-establish a relationship with him (reconciliation) by godly living, godly teaching, godly concern for others, and personal sacrifice.

Chapter 2

Mission and Missiology:
Concepts and Terms

All specialized fields of study develop their own unique vocabularies. This is necessary so individuals who specialize in that field can be precise as they carry out research and communicate with others involved in those disciplines. Missiology is no different. It is a technical field of study that makes use of a number of specialized terms. Understanding how the terms are used is crucial as you proceed in your missiological studies.

Mission – The Missio Dei

In general, the word *mission* (singular) is used differently than the word *missions* (plural). There is a good deal of history involved in the development of the technical terms. Scott Moreau has sketched a brief overview of that information (2000:636-638). The term *mission* refers to God's mission in his world. It involves the entire scope of God's activity in human history as he works to accomplish his purposes. God may use the church to assist him in accomplishing part of his mission in the world, but he is not restricted to working through the church. This is God's world. He has always worked independently of his people to accomplish his purposes. *Mission* does not refer to the specific things God may do in an individual's life, or even in the life of a church. Rather it has to do with the big picture of God's intentions for humanity.

McIntosh points out that the Latin term, *missio Dei*, literally means *"the sending of God,"* (2000:631-633). Some use the term in a comprehensive sense, referring to all that God does to accomplish the salvation of humankind, including all that he has asked the church to do in its missionary task. Others use the term to refer more specifically to God's purpose in salvation, carried out in the incarnation and atoning death of Jesus. Still others suggest that the term refers to God's overall purpose of bringing peace to the world. They suggest that what is going on in the world, then, defines or sets the agenda for the church. In this view, the church is God's tool for peace and harmony in the world rather than for the salvation of the lost. Since peace and harmony is the goal, evangelism becomes an inappropriate practice. I would reject this understanding of the *missio Dei*. God does want peace and harmony in his world. But he also wants his estranged children to be reconciled to him so both he and they can enjoy a loving relationship. For that to happen, the effects of sin must be eliminated by faith in the sacrifice of Jesus. The way to accomplish peace and harmony in the world is for all people to be restored to fellowship with God and learn to live in a way that reflects the image and glory of Go—which he has put into each of us.

As I use the term *missio Dei*, I refer primarily to God's overarching or primary mission in the world, his desire to see all people reconciled to himself. Secondarily, it may refer to how the church participates with God in accomplishing that purpose. But the main focus of the term is on God's purpose or mission, not on the church's activity in working with him to accomplishing that purpose.

Missions

If *mission* refers to God's primary mission in the world, then *missions* (plural) refers to what the church does in participating with God in accomplishing his mission in the world. Missions is the church going into the world, telling the story of Jesus and the possibility of reconciliation to God, which provides hope for an eternal home in heaven (Peters 1972:11). *Missions* is the sending of reconciled people to share the gospel with those who have not yet been reconciled to God. Bosch explains that:

> *[M]ission.* . . refers primarily to the *missio Dei* (God's mission), that is, God's self-revelation as the One who loves the world, God's involvement in and with the world, the nature and activity of God, which embraces both the church and the world, and in which the church is privileged to participate. *Missio Dei* enunciates the good news that God is a God-for-people. *Missions.* . . refer to particular forms, related to specific times, places, or needs, of participation in the *missio Dei* (1991:10).

The terminology can become confusing, however, because sometimes we refer to God's mission (as in the *missio Dei*) and also to the church's mission. Van Engen's definition of mission is not referring to the *missio Dei*, but to the church's mission, or to missions. Van Engen says,

> Mission is the people of God intentionally crossing barriers from church to nonchurch, faith to nonfaith, to proclaim by word and deed the coming of the kingdom of God in Jesus Christ; this task is achieved by means of the church's participation in God's mission of reconciling people to God, to themselves, to each other, and to the world, and gathering them into the church through repentance and faith in Jesus Christ by the work of the Holy Spirit with a view to the transformation of the world as a sign of the coming of the kingdom in Jesus Christ (1996:26-27).

Though the seeming inconsistent use of the terms mission and missions may at first be confusing, the context in which the terms are encountered will usually clarify their usage.

More important than whether Van Engen uses the singular or plural form of mission is the content of his definition. His focus is on the church's going into the world *in participation with God* in accomplishing God's goal of reconciling lost people to himself. This focus is essential if we are to have a biblical view of ourselves as missionaries in God's world.

But what is the scope of missions? Is it limited to preaching the good news? Or does missions include additional expressions of love and concern that might be classified as humanitarian aid, such as providing food, clothing, shelter, and medical attention for the poor or oppressed? Some understand missions to be limited to evangelistic efforts while others would include social services as legitimate missions activity.

A biblical response to the question is that missions involves both evangelism and concern for the well-being of others. Jesus' own ministry provides us with an example of loving concern for the whole person. During Jesus' ministry, hungry people were fed. Sick people were healed. Downtrodden people were lifted up. Marginalized people were validated. Helpless people were empowered. However, all of these things were done in a context of revelation and reconciliation—revealing God and assisting people in re-establishing a relationship with their heavenly Father. In the ministry of Jesus and the early church, the things we would define as social action were never divorced from evangelism. The two went hand in hand.

Maintaining a balance is difficult. Spiritual concerns are more important than physical concerns. But God is clearly concerned with physical needs. Humanitarian efforts are expensive. We want to help those in need, but we do not want to create the impression that we are offering humanitarian aid in exchange for a willingness to hear the gospel. We need to help those in need with a *no-strings-attached* attitude, and we need to tell the story of Jesus to everyone who will listen. Our missions must be *holistic*, addressing the needs of the whole person, for it is the whole person that is created in God's image.

Evangelism

Evangelism is preaching the gospel. Peters has a slightly more detailed definition. He say evangelism "refers to the initial phase of Christian ministry. It is the authoritative proclamation of the gospel of Jesus Christ as revealed in the Bible in relevant and intelligible terms, in a persuasive manner with the definite purpose of making Christian converts," (1972:11). Missions and evangelism are not synonymous terms. In fact, some believers do not see them as necessarily related. Andrew Kirk explains the problem.

> There is no consensus yet among people from different Christian traditions about the relation of evangelism to missions. Most separate the two, considering evangelism to be part of missions, i.e., an essential dimension of the total activity of the church. This division has been resisted by some—mostly from the conservative evangelical section of the Church—who believe that the Church's mission *is* evangelism, whereas the Church's diaconal ministries must be seen strictly as subordinate, a consequence of its evangelical commission (2000:56).

If we turn to the Bible for an answer we see that God's mission, and therefore our mission, is rooted in reconciliation,

21

which enables God and his human children to enjoy the relationship he had envisioned from the very beginning. Reconciliation and relationship can only happen if the good news of Jesus is told so people's sins can be washed away by the blood of Jesus as they respond in faith. From a very basic biblical perspective, evangelism *is* the church's mission. Yet as I have already pointed out, evangelism cannot be done in the presence of human need without those needs being addressed. If we allow the Bible to guide us in establishing our mission and ministry priorities, examining Jesus' own ministry as an example of how to go about mission and ministry, then loving concern for the physical needs of people created in God's image will also be part of our larger mission to the world. Evangelism will be combined with "social action" just as it was in Jesus' ministry, demonstrating God's concern for the whole person. Evangelism, therefore, is one aspect of missions.

Missiology

Johannes Verkuyl notes that:

> [M]issiology is the study of the salvation activities of the Father, Son, and Holy Spirit throughout the world geared toward bringing the kingdom of God into existence. Seen in this perspective, missiology is the study of the worldwide church's divine mandate to be ready to serve this God who is aiming his saving acts toward this world (1978:5).

Alan Neely has a slightly different perspective. He says, "missiology is the conscious, intentional, ongoing reflection on the doing of mission. It includes theory(ies) of mission, the study and teaching of mission, as well as the research, writing and publication of works regarding mission" (2000:633-635).

Neely's definition focuses on the academic aspect of the discipline while Verkuyl's focuses on the theological foundations of the discipline. Following Verkuyl's lead, a number of missiologists use the terms *missiology* and *theology of mission* (or mission theology) interchangeably. Their definitions of missiology grow out of the theological foundations of the discipline. Bosch and Van Engen are two leading missiologists who seem to do this (Bosch 1991:8-11; Van Engen 2000:949-951). This can be confusing. In my opinion, missiology and theology of mission are not the same thing and I do not believe it is wise to use the terms interchangeably.

Neely's definition of missiology that focuses on its academic nature as a discipline seems preferable. Missiology is the study of missions in the broad, general sense. It is an academic pursuit: reading, analyzing, reflecting, writing, discussing, theorizing. It includes the study of anthropology and ecclesiology, as well as theology. A foundational element in the field of missiology is the theology of mission, which, among other things, focuses on the theological foundations underlying the study and practice of missions. Obviously the two are very closely connected, but the terms should not to be used interchangeably.

Theology

Demarest suggests that theology is "an attempt to reduce religious truth to an organized system." He goes on however to offer a more detailed explanation:

> In greater detail theology might be defined as the discipline that (1) presents a unified formulation of truth concerning God and his relationship to humanity

and the universe as this is set forth in divine revelation and that (2) applies such truths to the entire range of human life and thought. Systematic theology thus begins with divine revelation in its entirety, applies the Spirit-illumined mind to comprehend the revelation, draws out the teachings of Scripture via sound grammatical-historical exegesis, provisionally respects the development of the doctrine of the church, orders the results in a coherent whole, and applies the results to the full scope of human endeavor (1984:1064-1065).

The word *theology*, is a combination of two words, *theos*, God and *logos*, word. Thus, theology is *words about God*, or thought and discussion (reflection) about God and spiritual things. Understood in this sense, theology has existed from the beginning of time, for theology is what humans have thought about God. Theology is not what the Bible says. Theology is what humans think about what the Bible says. Theology is our attempt to understand and apply the Scriptures.

Our theology today should be rooted in the ideas and information we find in Scripture. What did Jesus teach about God? What did Paul teach about God? When we reflect on God and spiritual things, and how those realities impact life, we are engaging the theological process, we are engaging in theology. It is important that our theology not be predicated on preconceived ideas or untested assumptions. There is no place for *a priori* reasoning[1] in theological reflection. Unfortunately, a great deal of theology is based on *a priori* reasoning or untested assumptions. Some theology is more closely

---

[1] *a priori* reasoning involves reaching a conclusion before examining the evidence, or examining evidence in a biased way with a conclusion already in mind so that the evidence leads one to the conclusion one had already reached.

associated with philosophy and logic than with the teachings of Scripture. This is not to say that philosophy and logic are bad. They are not. Philosophy and logic are useful tools for thoughtful investigation and analysis. But our reflection about God and spiritual things should grow primarily out of what we learn in the Scriptures. Exegesis of the biblical text should guide and inform our theology. Theological conclusion cannot precede exegesis.

What is the relationship between theology and missions? Unfortunately it has not always been what it should be. In the early days of Christianity, persecution united believers in their struggle to survive. But when Christianity became a legal religion under the rule of Constantine, the more relaxed atmosphere allowed believers to focus on matters other than survival. The result was the development of different theological positions on a number of significant issues. A major area of disagreement had to do with the nature of Jesus and his relation to the Father. Theological debate over the nature of Christ distracted the church for several centuries (McGrath 1997:5-24).

During this time, and for centuries to follow, missions outreach continued to be an important part of Christian activity, but it was not included in the developing theology of the church. Jesus' theological reflection had included the idea of missions outreach. He talked about it and trained his followers to do it, commanding them to *go and make disciples*. Missions was the guiding principle or foundational concept of Paul's theological reflection. He had been called to be a missionary and missions permeated all he thought and did. But over the centuries, as the church's theological reflection developed, missions (as part of the theology of the church) was conspicuously absent. The reason for this was understandable: early Christian theologians were discussing disagreements and responding to problems. Their writings reflect those concerns.

25

Missions was not an issue of dispute so it did not get addressed (Bromiley 1978:3). However, over the centuries, theologians continued to ignore missions as a fundamental reality of Christianity. The result of this unfortunate dichotomy was that missions became at best a secondary consideration. Missions was something some Christians were interested in, but it was not the heart and soul of the church. For many, Christianity involved a set of propositions to be believed rather than a story to be told.

By the late 1800's a number of theologians had become convinced that systematic theology no longer met the needs of the church because it was not thoroughly rooted in the text of Scripture. This dissatisfaction with systematic theology gave rise to a new approach to theology known as biblical theology (Reventlow 1992:483-505).

Biblical Theology

In the late 1800's and early 1900's the *movement* known as biblical theology developed as an alternative to systematic theology. Some conservative Christians, however, were uncomfortable with some of the theological assumptions of those who were leading the way in the new movement. They were considered too liberal. The idea, though, of an approach to theology that was thoroughly rooted in sound biblical exegesis was appealing. This eventually gave rise to the *process* or method known as biblical theology, which could be practiced without the theological assumptions with which some conservatives were uncomfortable (Enns 1989:19-24).

Rosner, who compares biblical theology to a construction site, says that, "The task of biblical theology is to present the teaching of the Bible about God and his relations to the world in a way that lets the biblical texts set the agenda" (2000:5). Childs offers a more detailed explanation:

This discipline has as its fundamental goal to understand the various voices within the whole of the Christian Bible, New and Old Testament alike, as a witness to the one Lord Jesus Christ, the selfsame divine reality. The Old Testament bears testimony to Christ who has not yet come; the New to the Christ who has appeared in the fulness of time. The two testaments do not relate to each other simply on the level of their role as witnesses. To remain on the textual level is to miss the key which unites dissident voices into a harmonious whole. Rather Biblical Theology attempts to hear the different voices in relation to the divine reality to which they point in such diverse ways (1992:85).

Childs is suggesting that the task of biblical theology is to weave together the various Christological threads contained in the Bible into a "tapestry" (Van Engen 1996:40-43) which allows us to view the larger picture of God's activity in human history. But biblical theology cannot simply report what the Bible says about God and spiritual matters, it must contextualize the information, making it useful and appropriate for believers today.

Biblical theology is a *process* which involves an approach to the Scriptures: 1) which understands God's communication as a unified whole, 2) which was revealed progressively in different times and cultures, 3) yet which contains a single integrative motif or metatheme, 4) through which God reveals his communicative intent to all people, 5) through individual authors who each reveal part of the whole message, 6) making their own individual theological reflection available, 7) for the individual to analyze and synthesize into a, 8) contextualized, culturally appropriate theology, 9) available for reflection and use by a faith community.

Figure 1 illustrates the process of biblical theology.

27

What is the relationship between missions and biblical theology? As pointed out earlier, systematic theology has not, generally speaking, found a place for missions in its synthesis of Christian doctrine. If one reads systematic theology, assuming it actually represented a systematic presentation of what the Bible had to say, one

---

SCRIPTURE

1. God's communication understood as a unified whole
2. Revealed progressively in different times and cultures
3. Yet containing a single integrating motif, a unifying metaheme
4. Through which God reveals his communicative intent
5. Through individual authors who reveal part of the whole message
6. Making their own theological reflection available
7. For individuals to analyze and synthesize
8. Into a contextualized, culturally appropriate theology
9. Available for reflection and use by a faith community

FIGURE 1: THE PROCESS OF BIBLICAL THEOLOGY

could conclude that missions was entirely unimportant. That is because systematic theology is not *chronologically* systematic. It does not begin at the beginning of the Bible and go through the Bible, allowing the historical context to determine the agenda. Systematic theology does not allow the metatheme of God's communication to come through loud and clear so that God can speak to us about his purpose and his goals. Biblical theology comes closer to doing that than does systematic theology. The process of biblical theology produces a theology that is rooted in God's mission in the world and our participation with him in that mission. The *missio Dei* comes through clearly and sharply when one allows Scripture to set the theological agenda.

28

Theology Of Mission

What is theology of mission, or mission theology? Andrew Kirk suggests that:

> The theology of mission is a disciplined study which deals with questions that arise when people of faith seek to understand and fulfill God's purposes in the world, as these are demonstrated in the ministry of Jesus Christ. It is a critical reflection on attitudes and actions adopted by Christians in pursuit of the missionary mandate. Its task is to validate, correct and establish on better foundations the entire practice of mission (2000:21).

Wilbert Shenk defines it from a slightly different perspective:

> Formally, mission theology is the effort to understand and interpret the *missio Dei* in light of Scripture, the experience of the church in mission throughout history, and the present sociopolitical context in order to give guidance to the church in fulfilling its missionary calling (2001:105).

I like Shenk's definition because it mentions how we understand and interpret God's mission in an attempt to fulfill our mission in the world.

In linking mission theology with biblical theology, Peters has said:

> Missionary theology is not an appendix to biblical theology; it belongs at its very core. No doctrine of God, Christ or the Holy Spirit has been

expounded completely according to the Bible until it has established the triune God as the outgoing God of mission, the God of saving purpose and relationship to mankind who undertakes a program for the progressive realization of His purpose (1972:27).

My own definition is that: *Theology of mission is reflection on the biblical missional mandate and the various cultural contexts in which we seek to participate with God in accomplishing his mission in the world today—the reconciliation of all people.*
Biblical theology illuminates God's mission in the world more brightly than other approaches. It helps us understand more clearly God's purpose in creation and his desire for a relationship with all people, which is the metatheme of his communication to us in the Scriptures. That metatheme, the missional thread in the tapestry of Scripture, is seen more clearly with a "biblical" approach than with a systematic approach. The missional metatheme that emerges so clearly in the Bible impacts the way we understand the establishment of the nation of Israel. It impacts the way we think about the incarnation and the death of Jesus. It impacts our understanding of reconciliation as God's goal for humanity. It impacts our understanding of our call to tell the story of Jesus so people can put their faith in him and enjoy a renewed relationship with God. Biblical theology provides the foundation for our reflection regarding our participation with God in his mission.

Our theological reflection about mission, however, must go beyond who we are and what we are supposed to do. It must also include *how* we can best do the job God has called us to do. That means our theology of mission will necessarily involve reflection 1) on the communication process, 2) on cultural concerns, and 3) on how to allow the gospel to take root in each native land in a way that is culturally appropriate

30

for a specific people group. To do those things effectively we need to reflect on how they have been done before. We need to analyze previous efforts to communicate the message effectively, contextualizing it to local cultures. We need to study the successes and failures of the church's past missionary outreach. Then we need to develop a plan of action and get busy. After a time of mission activity, we need to stop and reflect on what we have done. *Action-reflection-action*, is the three-pronged approach to successful missions activity.

In summary, theology of mission involves theology, but not only theology. It also involves anthropology, and mission history. It involves doing, analyzing what we have done, and doing some more, trying to improve on what we did before.

Incarnational Mission/Ministry

The concept of incarnational mission or ministry is crucial to success in proclaiming the gospel and ministering effectively to God's people in their unique sociocultural context. The idea of incarnational mission and ministry grows out of God's willingness to become human (the incarnation) in order to identify with us, communicate effectively with us, and serve us. In the prolog to his gospel, John tells us that the Word was not only with God but was God. The Word became a human being, living as one of us, revealing the Father to us (Jn. 1:1-18). The writer of the letter to the Hebrews explains the incarnation from a communication perspective when he says that in these last days God has spoken to us through his Son, who is the exact representation of his (God's) being. In his second letter to the believers in Corinth, Paul said that God was in Christ reconciling the world to himself (2 Cor. 5:19). Jesus explained his ministry by saying that he had not come to be served but to serve, and to give his life as a ransom for many (Mt. 20:28).

31

God carried on an incarnational mission/ministry when he became one of us in order to serve and save us. Paul spoke of becoming all things to all people in order to save them (1 Cor. 9:20-23). When Paul was with Jewish people he looked at life from a Jewish cultural perspective. He thought and acted like a Jew. When he was with people who were not Jewish, he looked at life from their point of view—from the perspective of a person who had no previous experience with God. What Paul was describing is what missiologists call *incarnational ministry*.

How do we accomplish incarnational mission/ministry? By "becoming" one of the people to whom we go. It is not possible for someone raised in one culture to become so much a part of another culture that they think and feel as do those who were born and raised in that culture. However, if one makes an effort to learn the language, learn the culture, associate and identify with the people as much as one can, he or she can gain enough insight and understanding into that culture to be accepted and trusted by the people of that culture.

Language learning is hard. It can be a frustrating and humiliating experience. Culture shock can have a devastating effect on us and our work if we allow it to drive us back into our houses or into the safety and shelter of the missionary community. (I will discuss both of these topics in more detail in a later chapter). For the time being, my point is that missionaries need to be *with* and *among* the people to whom they are communicating the Good News. Only in being with them can we learn about them and eventually become one of them. Only when we can identify with the people enough to see the world through their eyes can we minister to them effectively. Without an incarnational approach to missions and ministry we will simply be Western missionaries offering Western solutions to problems analyzed from a Western point of view. We will be, for the most part, irrelevant.

Summary

Mission, *Missio Dei*: God's overarching or primary mission in the world, his desire to see all people reconciled to himself.

Missions: Missions (plural) refers to what the church does in participating with God in accomplishing his mission in the world.

Evangelism: Evangelism is preaching the gospel, and will be combined with "social action" just as it was in Jesus' ministry to demonstrate God's concern for the whole person.

Missiology: Missiology is the study of God's mission and the church's missionary activity. It is an academic pursuit: reading, analyzing, reflecting, writing, discussing, theorizing. It includes the study of anthropology and of ecclesiastical history as well as theology.

Theology: Theology is reflection about God and spiritual things, and how those realities impact life.

Biblical Theology: Biblical theology is a *process* which involves an approach to the Scriptures: 1) which understands God's communication as a unified whole, 2) which was revealed progressively in different times and cultures, 3) yet which contains a single integrative motif or metatheme, 4) through which God reveals his communicative intent to all people, 5) through individual authors who each reveal part of the whole message, 6) making their own individual theological reflection available, 7) for the individual to analyze and synthesize into a 8) contextualized, culturally appropriate theology, 9) available for reflection and use by a faith community.

Theology of Mission: Theology of mission is reflection on the biblical missional mandate and the various cultural contexts in which we seek to participate with God in accomplishing his mission in the world today—the reconciliation of all people.

Incarnational Mission/Ministry: Incarnational mission or ministry involves becoming, as fully as possible, one of the people to whom you go to preach the gospel. It involves learning the culture and language of the local people so you can see the world through their eyes, seeing what they see from their point of view, so you can address their needs in a way that is relevant to them.

Part II

Mission Training

In this section, I will present an overview of the basic components of the study of missions, discussing what is involved in each element, and why each one is important and helpful in preparing God's people to serve him more effectively.

I will begin by explaining the three-part division of missiological studies: Word, World and Church, or biblical studies, anthropological studies, and ecclesial studies.

Biblical studies necessarily includes thinking about the hermeneutical process, exegesis (looking closely at the details) and biblical theology (analyzing the big picture perspective).

Anthropological studies include cultural studies, analyzing worldview, understanding the need for and approaches to contextualization, and cross-cultural communication.

Ecclesial studies include a study the missionary activity and expansion of the church, as well as the history of missions.

Each one of these disciplines is a field of study in which one can specialize. Since missiology is a multidisciplinary discipline, proficiency in each of them, and a great deal of proficiency in at least two of them, is essential. Like mission work itself, the study of missiology is not for the faint of heart. It is a difficult and demanding task requiring dedication, commitment, discipline and sacrifice.

Chapter 3

The Three-Part Division of Missiological Studies

As noted earlier, the three-part division of Word, World, and Church that is often used to explain the components of missiological studies was first used by Woodberry. The point is simple: to be effective in taking the word of God into the world, the church must understand the word, the world and herself (past and present). It is by the integration of these three areas of study, theology, anthropology and ecclesiology, that we prepare ourselves to effectively proclaim the word of God to the world.

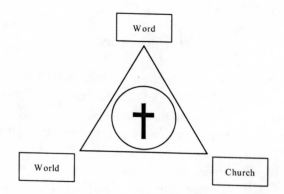

FIGURE 2: MISSIOLOGICAL INTEGRATION

Jesus is at the center of missiological thought and action. As we study the *word* (the Scriptures), we focus specifically on Jesus as God the Word who became God the Son, presenting us with the most complete expression of God available to humankind. As we study the *church*, we focus on the body of Christ as a tool in God's hand to accomplish his purpose in the world, and we focus on past missions efforts, reflecting on how to be more effective in the future. As we study the *world* (anthropology) we seek to understand other peoples, learning how to communicate with them in ways that were culturally appropriate so the story of Jesus will be relevant and meaningful to them.

It is the integration of these three areas of study that make missiology a unique and interesting discipline, lending itself to participation with God in accomplishing his purpose in the world.

Word (Theology)

The focus of this section will be on hermeneutics (how to study and interpret the Scriptures), textual studies (exegesis), and biblical theology.

Hermeneutics

The methodological process of interpreting and applying God's communication in the Scriptures is referred to as hermeneutics. The hermeneutical task is not an easy one. Thiselton provides a comprehensive description of the process:

> Hermeneutics may be defined as the theory of interpretation. More precisely, biblical hermeneutics inquires into the conditions under which the interpretation of the biblical texts may be judged possible, faithful, accurate, responsible, or productive in relation to some specified goal. Whereas exegesis involves the actual process of interpretation, biblical

hermeneutics moves beyond interpretation. It entails a study of method, inviting reflection on the nature, methods, and goals of biblical interpretation. It also draws on general hermeneutic theory, that is, on traditions of scholarship—within philosophy, the social sciences, theories of literature, and semiotics—that shed light on questions about meaning and understanding. The subject embodies a proper concern to understand the biblical writings not only as particular historical documents of the past but also as texts that address the present with a living and transforming voice. This has often been described as the task of "application," though some prefer to speak of "recontextualization." Finally, theological questions about the status and nature of the Bible also shape hermeneutics. Whether or in what sense the Bible is seen as the authoritative word of God shapes the ways in which issues are explored (1993:279).

Hermeneutics is an essential concern of the missionary enterprise. How will one know if he or she is interpreting and applying the Scriptures properly without analyzing the process of interpretation and application? This is especially true in missions, where we take the Scriptures, which we normally interpret and apply in our own cultural setting, to another cultural setting and attempt to interpret and apply them there. Unfortunately, missiologists, to a large degree, have left the subject of hermeneutics to theologians. Yet since the Scriptures were not originally communicated in our Western culture, every hermeneutical exercise is, in fact, a cross-cultural event. Who better to be involved in hermeneutics than missiologists?

Richard Longnecker has described and analyzed the

interpretive methods of the Jews, including Jesus and the early church (1975). His findings can be unsettling for those trained in the West, who assume that the way they were taught to interpret and apply Scripture is *the* one and only correct way to do so, and that God's people (including Jesus) must surely have used those same procedures, working out of the same basic methodological assumptions. They did not. Jesus and his followers interpreted the Scriptures out of a different methodological framework than we do—a framework with which many of us would be uncomfortable given our Western ways of interpreting the spoken and written word. As the cultural makeup of the church changed from predominantly Jewish to predominantly non-Jewish, interpretive methods also changed. Over the centuries, Western logic and scientific precision was applied to interpretive methodology and the approach to interpretation with which we are now comfortable was developed.

How does this relate to missiological studies? Awareness of hermeneutical issues is important in missiological studies because people of other cultures, with worldviews different from our own, may approach the interpretation and application of Scriptures differently than we do. Our Western rules for interpreting and applying Scripture may seem foreign and confusing, unnatural and unnecessarily complicated to them. It may be that their hermeneutical methodology (even if they are unaware of having one) may be more like the first century Jewish methodology that Jesus and his followers used than is our own.

The way we do things in the West is not the only way to do them. The way we interpret and apply Scripture is not the only way to do it. Being aware of hermeneutical issues helps us understand this. It also helps us understand the importance (and the difficulty) of contextualization when we are trying to preach and teach the eternal truths of God's word in culturally appropriate ways in a cultural context different from our own and different from the cultures represented within the pages of Scripture.

Textual Studies

Textual studies refers to the detailed analysis of the biblical text. But the details should always be analyzed with the big picture panoramic view of the underlying metatheme of Scripture in mind. If we study the details of God's communication to us in isolation from the basic point of his communication (his desire for a relationship with all people), we have no frame of reference for understanding the details. In other words, if we attempt to interpret the details of any text apart from the overall context to which those details are related, we have no chance of interpreting them correctly.

To analyze a text in order to understand what the text says is *exegesis*. The practical goal of exegesis is to produce useful interpretations of the biblical text (Stuart 1992:Vol. 2, 682-688). Some exegetes propose that the goal is to find out what the original message meant to the original receptors without any responsibility for applying the text in a contemporary setting. I believe that is doing only half the job. It is vitally important to attempt to discover, as far as possible, what the text meant to the original receptors. But the reason that is important is to enable us to make a contemporary application that is consistent with the author's original intent.[2] Interpretation and application go together. Interpretation without application is useless. Application without interpretation is irresponsible.

However, it is important to remember that after exegesis

---

[2]In saying this I am aware that I am betraying my bias toward a thoroughgoing Western hermeneutic rooted in historical-grammatical exegesis.

is completed and we understand the text in its historical setting (and our understanding is partial at best), how that text is applied will vary depending on the contemporary setting under consideration. Textual studies for the missiologist is more complicated than textual studies for a typical Western theologian. The missiologist must have the same exegetical skills as the theologian, but he or she must also understand how to apply the text contextually, depending on the culture in which he or she is working.

Biblical Theology

As I discussed in the previous chapter, biblical theology is a process. It approaches the Bible as God's communication to humans, containing a unified message that must be taken into consideration when analyzing the individual sections within Scripture. The task is to weave together the various Christological threads contained in the Bible into a tapestry which allows us to view the larger picture of God's activity in human history. Childs sees biblical theology as the vehicle that performs this integrative task as well as the contextualization of the integrated presentation to various contemporary settings.

There is another essential part of the reflective enterprise of Biblical Theology that moves the discipline even more closely into the theological arena. Biblical Theology seeks not only to pursue the nature of the one divine reality among the various biblical voices, it also wrestles theologically with the relation between the reality testified to in the Bible and that living reality known and experienced as the exalted Christ through the Holy Spirit within the present community of faith. These two vehicles of revelation—Word and Spirit—are neither to be identified, nor are they to be separated and played one against the other. . . [T]he divine imperatives are no longer moored in the past, but continue to confront the hearer in the present as truth. Therefore it is constitutive of Biblical Theology that it be normative and not merely descriptive, and that it be responsive to the imperatives of the present and not just of the past (1992:86).

Biblical theology must not only discover and report what was believed in the past, it must also integrate the various themes and motifs of Scripture, contextualizing them for believers today for use in whatever cultural setting their faith community may exist.

When we use the process of biblical theology to analyze the various themes and motifs of Scripture (covenant or kingdom, for example), along with the symbolic language used to explain and illustrate God's communicative intent (metaphors which highlight relationship, such as shepherd/sheep, father/child, husband/wife), weaving them together into a unified whole, we find that they are rooted in the metatheme of God's desire for a relationship with all people. We also find that God's basic mission in this world is to offer reconciliation to each person so the divine-human relationship broken by sin can be restored.

The various components of biblical studies give us a clear understanding of God's mission in the world, his expectation of our participation with him in accomplishing that mission, and insight into the complexity of delivering his message in a culturally appropriate way to people around the world. Biblical studies, including hermeneutics, textual studies and biblical theology are integral to the study of missions.

World (Anthropology)

Jacob Lowen tells the following story about an interesting conversation he once had:

> A group of Lengua Indians was sitting around a fire outside one of the newly erected temporary shelters in a recently settled village in Paraguay. The group was in the process of changing its nomadic hunting way of life to one of sedentary agriculture.
>
> The author, sitting with them, was making an anthropological investigation of the situation, hoping to find ways and means to facilitate this difficult transition for the tribes. He had been entertaining the group with accounts of his early missionary experiences among the Choco Indians of Colombia. Among other things he had told them about some of the cultural errors he had made when he first tried to reach that tribe with the gospel. After exposing his own mistakes at some length, he suddenly stopped and asked, "Have the missionaries who brought you the message about Jesus Christ also made mistakes like this?"
>
> A painful silence followed. It was finally broken by the host who felt obligated to answer. "It is very hard for Lengua Indians to say if the missionaries have or have not made mistakes." The visiting anthropologist well understood the truth of this assertion, for the Lengua concept of the "good innermost," did make it difficult to criticize others. However, not wanting to lose this excellent occasions for discovering some of the attitudes of the Lengua toward the existing missionary program, he continued to press: "Maybe you could mention at least one of the areas in which there have been mistakes." After

another period of silence the host answered in the low German vernacular highly influenced by Lengua syntax, "*Es krautze woa nich es yeiche*," which freely translated said, "They scratched where it doesn't itch" (1975:3).

I have included this lengthy quote to illustrate a point: when we go into a culture with our own agenda regarding the needs of the people, or our own solutions to what we perceive their problems to be, we will not be able to address their needs effectively. We will be scratching where it doesn't itch.

Everyone needs to hear the gospel. But they need to hear it in a way that is relevant to their culture, in a way that makes sense to them. The questions we ask may not be the same questions the people of another culture are asking. They may ask a similar question, but not the same question. And their way of thinking about that similar question may be very different than the way we think about the questions we ask. For instance, I had been in Nigeria about six weeks. I was teaching at a Christian college and had been assigned to teach an undergraduate class on Paul's letters to the Corinthians. It was a large class of about eighty students.

Over the past few weeks I had noticed that questions related to difficulties seemed to focus on *who* caused them to happen rather than the less personal Western question related to *why* bad things happen. A question like this came up in class. Someone noticed that something bad had happened in Corinth and had asked who caused it to happen. I decided to take the opportunity to explain that many things simply happen and that often there was not a "*who*" to blame or to identify as the cause.

To illustrate my point I asked how many of them had ridden a bicycle down a dirt road or path. Nearly eighty hands went up. "Now," I said, "how many of you have hit a soft, sandy spot in the road, lost control of the bike and fallen over?" Again nearly eighty hands went up. "All right," I said, "why did that happen?" The class assembled in the large tin roofed open-air chapel was absolutely still. Eighty sets of eyes stirred at me in anticipation. I was about to explain a great mystery to them. I wanted to set it up again so no one would miss my point. I said, "Okay, you are riding down the road, peddling fast and everything is fine. Then suddenly you hit a spot of soft sand. The bicycle slows immediately. You are thrown forward. The front wheel begins to wobble. You lose your balance and fall down. Now why did that happen?" They waited. I hesitated. "Physics," I said triumphantly. And all eighty of them broke into laughter as if it was the funniest thing they had ever heard.

Their response caught me off guard. I wondered why they were laughing. I must not have explained it properly. I had not given them enough information. Surely, with enough scientific information they would see my point.

When the laughter died down, I began again. This time I explained in more detail. I explained about the forward momentum, the weight of the rider, the rotation of the wheels, the speed, the sudden slowing due to the impaired rotation of the front tire mired in the soft sand, inertia, balance, gravity. I explained it all. For someone who had never actually taken a physics class I thought I did an exceptional job. Then I asked again, "Why did you fall?" Again the waited with anxious anticipation. Again I said, "Physics." It was so clear. Surely they would understand. Again, all eighty of them burst into laughter. I was shocked and confused.

When the laughter died down I asked, "Why are you laughing?" From the back of the chapel a commanding voice from one of the older men asked, "Why are you telling us physics did it?" I had no answer. And I realized for the first time that I was in a very different place. It was not just the food, the dress, the climate, and other surface-level realities that, in the final analysis, were not really important. These people understood the world differently than I did. They were asking different questions than I asked, out of a framework that was completely unfamiliar to me. I was supposed to be their teacher. Yet it was becoming clear to me that I was first going to have to become the student before I could be effective as a teacher.

Missionaries and missiologists must be students. One of the most important things for missions students to study is anthropology. Anthropology is the study of human beings. Cultural anthropology should be a major component of study for all missionaries.

Culture

Paul Hiebert defines culture as, "the more or less integrated systems of ideas, feelings, and values and their associated patterns of behavior and products shared by a group of people who organize and regulate what they think, feel, and do," (1985:30). Charles Kraft defines it as, "a society's complex, integrated coping mechanism, consisting of learned, patterned concepts and behavior, plus their underlying perspectives (worldview) and the resulting artifacts (material culture)," (1996:38).

In the simplest terms, culture is everything about a group of people: their unconscious assumptions about reality that allow them to understand and organize their world, the behaviors, and social structures that allow them to go about their daily lives. The way people dress is part of their culture. So is the language they speak, the food they eat, the way houses are designed, the way children are raised, the way people see themselves in relation to the family and community, the educational system, music, art, the way business is conducted, religion, attitudes toward family members who have died, government, the roles of men and women in society. On and on the list could go. Culture is who we are as a people.

Culture is that which defines and differentiates one group of people from another. Within a basic cultural group, such as

47

Western culture (North America and Western Europe), there are subcultures. America, England and France are part of a broad cultural base known as Western culture. But America, England and France each have their own distinct cultures. Even though Americans and the British both speak English, there are significant cultural differences between the two groups of people. Even in America, there are distinct subcultures. Regional distinctions exist between the Northeast, the South, the Southwest and the Northwest. Food is different in these regions. Clothing styles may vary, as may the way one greets someone on the street. The English spoken by the typical person from Boston does not sound like the English spoken by the typical person from Mississippi.

Culture can be a difficult hurdle to overcome when presenting the gospel. Kraft tells of an encounter he had with the people of a tribe in North-central Nigeria who wondered what was wrong with Jesus. Kraft responded that there was nothing wrong with Jesus. Why, then, the people wanted to know, was he a shepherd? In their culture, the job of shepherding was reserved for young boys or people who were considered mentally incompetent. Jesus was obviously not a young boy, so was he mentally incompetent? Their tribal culture was so different from first century Jewish culture that they could not understand some of Jesus' behavior (1996:25).

R. Daniel Shaw tells of a problem encountered by missionaries in a village in Papua New Guinea. The people did not seem to be taking Christianity seriously. Even after the Scriptures had been translated into their language so they could read and study for themselves, the people did not give it the serious consideration it deserved.

Shaw was called in as a consultant, and began to investigate. After a number of casual conversations around the village he began to understand what had happened. In that particular tribe when someone was upset with someone else, the custom was for the person who was upset to ease the tension by standing in the middle of the village berating the person with whom he or she was upset. The things the unhappy person might say could sound positive, but would be laced with sarcasm. For instance, if John was upset about a trade he had made with Bill, he would stand in the center of the village and loudly proclaim "Bill is an honest and trustworthy businessman who always trades fairly. The goat I acquired from Bill died after only two but that is of not consequence. Bill is a trustworthy man and you can always trust him to deal honestly with you."

People in the village did not pay much attention to such displays of annoyance and dissatisfaction, for they knew the individual was simply letting off some steam.

Years before, when the first missionaries arrived, since they had no church building, they used to stand in the middle of the village and preach. The villages found it difficult to attach a great deal of significance to their words, since in their culture what the missionaries were doing was simply letting off some steam. So even when the Scriptures were translated for the people, they did not take the whole thing too seriously (Shaw & Van Engen 2000:156). The missionaries who had gone to that tribe sabotaged their own work by not understanding the culture in which they were sharing the Good News about Jesus.

Many cultures are represented within the pages of Scripture. When the portion of Scripture being studied represents a culture that in some ways is very different from the culture of the people studying the Scriptures, misunderstandings can occur. One day in Nigeria, in a class I was teaching on the gospels, students were confused at something Jesus said. The text was Lk. 14:28, where Jesus discussed building a tower without first counting the cost. Jesus said that if you begin to build and cannot finish, people would laugh at you. The students were confused by Jesus'

49

statement. Why would people laugh? This was very serious to these Bible students. It involved something Jesus said would happen. It was in the Bible. But what Jesus spoke about did not seem to match up with their experience. The problem was one of cultural expectation and procedure. In first century Jewish culture, planning was very important. You did not start a project until you had sufficient resources to finish the project. You saved your money until you could begin *and* finish the job. In Nigeria, however, the custom is different. If you come into some money and have a dream of building something, you use the money you have to begin the project. If you run out, you simply wait until you have more and then resume construction. Sometimes it is many months or even several years before additional funds are available to continue building. But at least you have begun. There is pride in having begun and no embarrassment in not being able to finish right away. Eventually the building will be built. The confusion my students experienced was due to cultural differences between their culture and that of Jesus' day.

There are people groups in Papua New Guinea who have never seen a sheep and do not understand the term shepherd. They are pig herders. How does one explain Jesus and the shepherd of the sheep to people who know nothing of sheep or shepherds? Do we compare Jesus to a pig herder? The job is very similar. So why not? If we describe Jesus as a pig herder, how will we explain the aversion the Jews had to pigs (Nida and Reyburn 1981:1)?

The point of all of these examples is simple: when we go into other cultures we must be aware of how different those cultures are from our own, and from the cultures represented in Scripture. We must be aware of those differences as we work among those people. Studying anthropology helps us analyze our own culture and our cultural assumptions, as well as learning about the cultural practices and assumptions of other groups of people. It prepares us to go into another culture and learn how those people think and live so we can teach them about Jesus in ways that makes sense to them, in ways that address the issues that they believe are important, so we will not be guilty of scratching where it does not itch.

Worldview

One of the most important parts of cultural studies is the study of worldview. Louis Luzbetak says:

> A world view represents the deepest questions one might ask about the world and life, and about the corresponding orientation that one should take toward them. More concretely, the world view provides answers to such basic questions as: Who or what am I? Why am I in the world? What is reality? How do humans differ from nonhumans (animals, objects, the invisible beings)? Who belongs to the invisible world and what are the invisible forces in the world? What is the proper orientation to time and space? What about life after death? What in life or the world is desirable or undesirable, and to what degree? (1988:252).

Hiebert explains worldview this way:

> Behind the observable patterns of human cultures seem to lie certain assumptions about the way the world is put together. Some of these assumptions, called "existential postulates," deal with the nature of reality, the organization of the universe, and the ends and purpose of human life. Others, values and norms, differentiate between good and evil, right and wrong. Some of these assumptions are made explicit in the beliefs and myths of the people. Others appear to the

51

anthropologist to be implicit in people's behavior. Taken together, the assumptions the anthropologist uses to explain a people's total response to their universe are sometimes called a "world view" (1983:356).

Kraft explains worldview as:

[T]he culturally structured assumptions, values, and commitments/allegiances underlying a people's perception of reality and their responses to those perceptions. Worldview is not separate from culture. It is included in culture as the structuring of the deepest-level presuppositions on the basis of which people live their lives (1996:52).

Figure 3 illustrates what Kraft, Hiebert and Luzbetak have suggested:

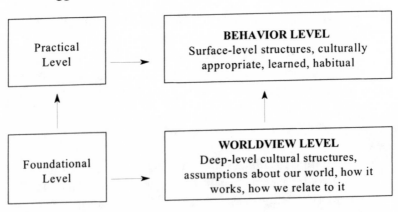

FIGURE 3: DEEP-LEVEL WORLDVIEW ASSUMPTIONS
(Adapted from Kraft 2000:1.2)

Worldview (normally written as one word rather than two) is made up of several *"universals,"* that is, things present in or functions of each worldview. Kraft discusses six worldview universals (1996:63-65):

1. *Classification:* People classify things in their world according to their worldview. Everything in a person's world—plants, animals, people, social institutions, supernatural beings, and so forth—fall into various worldview categories or classifications. A different worldview will result in different basis for classification.

2. *People or Groups*: People exist in relationship to other people or groups of people. We will relate to them, for instance, from or out of a group orientation or an individualistic orientation. Our worldview determines which orientation we will have.

3. *Causality*: How or why do things happen? What is the cause behind things that happen in the world? Are the laws of physics responsible, or are spiritual powers involved? Is it luck, fate, karma, an impersonal force, or a personal being or beings that cause what happens? Our worldview determines how we define causality in our world.

4. *Time*: Whether we have a linear or circular view of time, whether we are time oriented or event oriented, whether we focus most of our attention on the future, the present or the past, all depend on our worldview.

5. *Space*: How we arrange buildings, what shape they are, how big they are, what we put in them, how we arrange ourselves for eating, sleeping, working, how we think in terms of our relationship to nature (is it ours to use or are we part of it?) and the universe as a whole has to do with our worldview orientation.

6. *Relationship*: We must relate to the world around us. There is "us" (self) and there is everything and everyone else. How we relate to all those other things and people is rooted in our worldview. This category includes people and groups, but also includes everything else. How, for

instance, do we relate to animals or nature in general? What is our relationship to everything outside of ourselves?

These worldview universals are part of our deep-level, unconscious assumptions about the world we live in. Surface-level cultural behaviors and structures grow out of these deep-level unconscious assumptions. Surface-level behaviors and structures include things such as economics, politics, religion, social relationships, material culture, family, education, language, and much more (Kraft 2000:6.4). Religious practices are part of our surface-level behaviors that grow out of our deep-level unconscious assumptions about the world we live in. They grow out of our assumptions about causality. Why do things happen? What is the cause behind events in this world? Do things happen naturally, because of the laws of physics? Or are there supernatural forces at work behind the events that occur around us? Or, is there a third alternative that acknowledges both natural and supernatural forces, acknowledging that the ultimate "cause" is supernatural? For those who assume a supernatural cause, does their view include a single omnipotent being, or many gods and spirits who are part of the cause/effect equation in their worldview? One's surface-level religious behaviors or practices grow out of one's deep-level unconscious assumptions about causality.

Why is it important for missionaries to study worldview? If the religious faith of individuals or a group of people is rooted in their worldview, we must understand their worldview and know how to address worldview issues if we are to be successful in helping them come to faith in God and Jesus. If we believe they need to change their religious thinking, we need to understand why they think the way they do and how to go about discussing the subject in a way that will make sense to them.

Just as a side note, we sometimes hear people refer to a biblical or Christian worldview. You can see, however, from

Kraft's list of worldview universals that worldview involves areas of one's life that would not be included in one's faith orientation. All people who are Christians will have beliefs in common regarding God and how he wants us to live in this world. They will share a common perspective of basic values and morals, of right and wrong. Those *perspectives* would be included in worldview, but would not make up a person's total worldview. For instance, worldview includes our view of time and space. Do all Christians have to have the same orientation to time and space? Of course not. Americans are very *time oriented*. Punctuality is important to us. From our perspective, events should begin and end on time. Many non-Western people, however, are *event oriented*. The event (whatever it is—worship, wedding, funeral, council meeting) begins when it begins and it ends when it ends. Which view of time is Christian or biblical? Neither. Western people sleep in beds in separate rooms depending on age, gender and relationships. Husbands and wives sleep together. Siblings may sleep together, depending on gender and age for a period of time. Many non-Western people groups have quite different sleeping habits. In Papua New Guinea, for instance, the men of a Samo village sleep in separate areas of the communal *longhouse*, in specified arrangements depending on social ranking (marital status, age, importance), while the women sleep elsewhere (Shaw 1990:36). Does the Bible tell believers how they must arrange themselves for sleeping? Certainly not. Yet sleeping arrangements are part of one's worldview orientation regarding space. Worldview is much broader than one's Christian perspective.

Matters of faith are part of one's worldview, but do not represent all of one's worldview. It is not accurate, therefore (from a technical anthropological perspective), to refer to a biblical or Christian worldview. Believers in Africa and in America share a common faith and a common perspective on matters of faith. However, believers in

Africa and believers in America have very different worldviews. What people are attempting to describe when they refer to a Christian worldview exists, but the term worldview is not the best term to use in describing it. Worldview is a technical anthropological term that has to do with one's deep-level unconscious assumptions about reality. A Christian perspective on life is only one part of one's overall worldview. Technically speaking, we need to speak in terms of a *Christian perspective* rather than a Christian worldview.

Contextualization/Ethnotheologizing

Stephen Grunlan and Marvin Mayers observe that:

> Although we refer to Christianity as biblical Christianity, we must realize that it is never found apart from a culture; it is always a part of culture. The Christianity of the New Testament was a part of the culture of the Greco-Roman world of the first century. Today we find American Christianity, Colombian Christianity, and Nigerian Christianity. There is no such thing as plain Christianity. Christianity always expresses itself through a culture. It is unique in that it can be expressed equally well in any culture. It is the one religion that can meet people's needs in any society. (1988:230)

Sherwood Lingenfelter begins his book, *Transforming Culture*, by discussing two worship experiences he had in Cameroon, West Africa, with other worship experiences he has had in Europe, Latin America and Asia (1998:11-12). His point is that aside from encountering an occasional language barrier, Christian worship assemblies around the world are very similar to Western worship assemblies. Sometimes the only thing in those cultures that may resemble anything Western may be related to how they practice their Christian faith. They construct a rectangle building and sit on benches in rows with a preacher in front, preaching a lesson. The way they do things in that Western style worship assembly (sit, communicate, interact with one another) may not resemble the way they do anything else in their culture. But that is how they have learned to have a Christian worship assembly. Why is that? Because we have assumed that the way we "do church" is the way it should be done. Such thinking is *ethnocentric*—thinking that is centered in our own ethnic (cultural) thinking and practices.

Ethnocentrism is a natural human response. The way we do things seems right to us. But ethnocentrism is unacceptable in a cross-cultural or multi-ethnic setting. That is why it is important for missionaries to learn to *contextualize*, to practice *ethnotheologizing*.

What is contextualization? Dean Gilliland says:

> There is no single or broadly accepted definition of contextualization. The goal of contextualization perhaps best defines what it is. That goal is to enable, insofar as it is humanly possible, an understanding of what it means that Jesus Christ, the Word, is authentically experienced in each and every human situation. Contextualization means that the Word must dwell among all families of humankind today as truly as Jesus lived among his own kin. The gospel is Good News when it provides answers for a particular people living in a particular place at a particular time. This means the worldview of that people provides a framework for communication. The questions and needs of that people are a guide to the emphasis of the message, and the cultural gifts of that people become the medium of expression.
>
> Contextualization in mission is the effort made

by a particular church to experience the gospel for its own life in light of the Word of God. In the process of contextualization the church, through the Holy Spirit, continually challenges, incorporates, and transforms elements of the culture in order to bring them under the lordship of Christ (2000:225).

Contextualizing the gospel does not involve changing the gospel in any way, adding anything to it or deleting anything from it. Instead, contextualization means telling the authentic story of Jesus in a way that will be clear and understandable, culturally appropriate and accessible to the people of a given culture. Contextualization is what Paul was talking about in 1 Cor. 9:19-23.

> I make myself a slave to everyone, to win as many as possible. To the Jews I became like a Jew, to win the Jews. To those under the law I became like one under the law (though I myself am not under the law), so as to win those under the law. To those not having the law I became like one not having the law (though I am not free from God's law but am under Christ's law), so as to win those not having the law. To the weak I became weak, to win the weak. I have become all things to all men so that by all possible means I might save some. I do all this for the sake of the gospel, that I may share in its blessings.

Paul put himself in the place of the people with whom he was working at any given moment. When he worked with Jewish people he thought like a Jew (which was not hard for him). He thought about things from the perspective of Jewish culture, which included a long tradition of messianic promise and hope. He worked out of a Jewish worldview, preaching the gospel to them in a way that fit with their Jewish worldview.

However, when Paul worked with non-Jewish people he tried to think about life from their point of view. He adopted (as much as possible) their worldview, preaching and teaching from a Hellenistic cultural perspective. He did not preach a different gospel. He preached the same gospel in a different way, or from a different point of view. A comparison of Paul's sermon in Acts 13 to a Jewish audience and his sermon in Acts 17 to a non-Jewish audience is an example of contextualization.

In Acts 13, when preaching to a Jewish audience, Paul used the Old Testament Scriptures to make and support his arguments that Jesus was the fulfillment of prophecy—something a Jewish audience would be very interested in. However, in Acts 17, when preaching to a non-Jewish audience, Paul did not refer to the Jewish Scriptures or prophecy. Why not? At that point, his audience was not interested in what the Jewish Scriptures had to say. Rather, Paul began with a topic that interested his audience. By the time he finished his sermon, Paul had introduced God, Jesus, the resurrection and judgement. He preached the gospel to them. But he did it in a way that was relevant to *them*.

Contextualization is not only something that must be done as the gospel is preached. As the Christian faith takes root in a culture, it must be completely authentic to that culture. Jesus did not intend that Christianity be a Jewish faith (or an American faith) that is transplanted into other cultures. It is to be a faith that becomes native to each place where it is planted. To state this metaphorically, Christianity must be planted in the local soil of each culture, take root and grow into a plant that is native to that culture.

This means that contextualization must continue to occur after the initial stages of presentation. It must be an ongoing reality in the life of the church in each culture. This is what Kraft refers to as *ethnotheologizing*, the ongoing development of theology in and for each culture to make the Christian faith culturally appropriate and authentic in and for each people group.

Theology is not static. It is never finished. Each group of people who encounter Jesus in the Good News of the gospel must reflect about God and godly living in ways that are appropriate for them as a group of people. How can this be accomplished? Paul Hiebert has suggested a method that he calls *critical contextualization* (1994:88-90).

The critical method, as Hiebert outlines it, includes four steps. The first step in the critical contextualization process is *an exegesis of the culture*. The missionary, working with local church leaders, leads Christians in an *uncritical* examination of the local culture. They discuss beliefs and customs related to those beliefs without criticizing them. The goal of this first stage is to catalog features of the culture, not to analyze or critique them. What do the people believe and what do those beliefs lead them to do? What is involved, for instance, in their marriage traditions: selecting a mate, courtship, marriage, and beginning a family. What rites are associated with the birth of children? What do they mean? What about coming of age ceremonies? What are the rites and ceremonies related to death and burial? What do they mean? Note, this process can take months to complete.

After the culture has been cataloged, it is time for step two: *the exegesis of Scripture and the hermeneutical bridge*. The missionary leads the church in a study of the Scriptures related to the cultural traditions being considered. The missionary must be aware of his or her own cultural blind spots. He or she must be determined not to bring his cultural understanding of a text into this new cultural situation. To do this the missionary must be able to explain the historical setting of the text without adding a Western perspective to his explanation.

The missionary must also be able to explain the difference

between the *supracultural* truths of Scripture and the original cultural setting through which those truths were (are) communicated. Supracultural truths are truths or realities that exist outside or above culture. For instance, the truth being communicated in the command to greet one another with a holy kiss (Rom. 16:16) has to do with a warm, friendly greeting for brothers and sisters in Christ. In first century Hellenistic and Jewish culture the greeting was accomplished with a chaste brotherly or sisterly kiss. In some cultures, however, Christians kissing each other (chaste or not) would not be culturally appropriate. Therefore, the culturally specific command to kiss need not be carried over into each culture. But the idea of a warm friendly greeting for fellow believers must find expression. What would be an appropriate greeting for believers in the new culture? The missionary leading the church in Bible study must be able to make these kinds of distinctions each time culture is involved in the expression of a supracultural command or principle.

It is crucial that the church understand the difference between supracultural truths and the way those truths were applied or lived out in the original historical-cultural setting of the early Christian communities. Only then will the local church be equipped to develop a truly culturally appropriate yet completely biblical theology. This is what is meant by the *hermeneutical bridge*—the cultural application that grows out of an understanding of what the Bible says about a specific topic or issue.

The third step in the critical contextualization process is *the critical analysis of culture in light of biblical teachings*. This is done by the people themselves in a corporate setting with the missionary serving as an observer and advisor. The people discuss their own cultural practices in light of what they understand God's word to teach. The Holy Spirit plays a major role in the process at this point, helping the people understand

and apply the Scriptures appropriately in their cultural context. Missionaries must resist the temptation to tell the local people what to do or how to do it. That is not the missionary's job. That is the Holy Spirit's job. The reason so many churches around the world look like Western churches is that missionaries have been telling local people what to do and how to do it.

The real strength of the critical contextualization model and the key to a truly contextualized theology, is that the people who understand their culture better than anyone else are the ones to analyze it and, in light of God's word, with the help of the Holy Spirit, decide what aspects of their culture can be kept, what parts must be abandoned, and what parts can be modified to work within a biblical framework. Missionaries can ask questions if they think the people have overlooked some aspect of an issue. But they must remember that they do not fully understand the culture and should accept the judgement of those who do as to the appropriateness of a custom or tradition. Even if a specific custom or tradition (such as the amount of clothing that may or may not be worn by a native people) results in a negative emotional response for the missionary, he or she must not allow Western cultural conditioning to become a factor in the critique of the culture.[3]

Once the cultural critique is completed, step four includes *developing new biblical based customs to replace the ones that were abandoned.* Here again the missionary must resist the temptation to make suggestions, to say, "in America we do

---

[3] In the West, for instance, it is often assumed that when God made clothes for Adam and Eve to wear (Gen. 3:21), the outfit for Eve was designed in such a way so that her breasts were covered. Such an assumption is unwarranted. Nothing in the text suggests that Eve's breasts were covered. Our understanding of the text includes her breasts being covered because of our cultural conditioning, not because of what the text actually says.

it this way. . . ." If the new customs are to be truly contextualized, they must not be rooted in Western culture, but in the local culture. The people need to develop their own new Christian customs.

The critical contextualization method was specifically developed to aid Christians in the development of locally authentic theologies. In my opinion, it is the model best suited for use by cultural insiders in evaluating their own culture in light of biblical teaching and adjusting their cultural traditions and customs to comply with those teachings.

The critical method of contextualization must be combined with an anthropologically informed approach to the Scriptures to be effective.

A willingness to contextualize grows out of an awareness that *perception depends on perspective*. The missionary contextualizes the gospel (presentation) based on his or her understanding of the target culture. As contextualization continues, the new believers, who understand their culture better than the missionary ever will, must take the lead in contextualizing the church. The missionary must work with them, helping them understand the Scriptures, but if the church is to be culturally authentic it must be of the people not of the missionary.

As you can see from this brief overview, contextualization is a complex concept and process. Studying it is an essential part of missions training. Appendix A contains a list of books on anthropology and contextualization.

Cross-Cultural Communication

How many times in a conversation with someone else have you had to say, "That's not what I meant"? Communication between people of the same culture is not easy. Differences in age, gender, background, education, experience, language skills and many other things make communication between people of the same culture a challenging task. Communication across cultural boundaries is even more difficult.

Communication is a process that involves a number of complicated steps. A communicator must have an idea that he or she wants to communicate to a receptor. I will call the communicator C and the receptor R. In the communication process, C must conceive of a message to send to R. C must try to anticipate how R will interpret the message (infer meaning) as he or she receives it. What does C know about R's background, experiences, language skills, (and a host of other things) that will help C *encode* the message (put it into words) in a way that will allow R to get C's point? Taking all of those things into consideration, C must then encode the message and send it to R using linguistic symbols (words). R must realize that C has a point to make and must consider C's background, experiences, language skills, and so forth as he or she receives the incoming message and begins to *decode* and interpret it. If the message seems relevant to R, R will continue the decoding process and attach or infer meanings to the linguistic symbols being received. R will assume that the meanings he or she attaches to C's linguistic symbols are the same meanings C attached when selecting and sending them. If the meanings R attaches to the incoming symbols are similar to the ones C attached to them as he or she sent them, then R and C will communicate. If R attaches meanings different from the meanings C attached they will not communicate. From C's point of view, R will have *"misunderstood."* From R's point of view, C will have failed to make himself or herself clear.

As you can see, the communication process is one of encoding and decoding in which communicators must attempt to anticipate receptors' response. Meaning is inferred by receptors. The closer the relationship between the communicator and the receptor, the easier the process is. Figure 4 illustrates an eight-step communication process that I call the CIR model of communication. CIR stands for *code-inferential-relational* (Rogers 2002:17-60):

This process becomes even more complicated when attempted in a cross-cultural setting. David Hesselgrave suggests seven "dimensions" of cross-cultural communication (1991:164). They include: 1) *worldview*—ways of perceiving the world, 2) *cognitive processes*—ways of thinking, 3) *linguistic forms*—ways of expressing ideas, 4) *behavioral patterns*—ways of acting, 5) *social structures*—ways of interacting, 6) *media influence*—ways of channeling messages, 7) *motivational resources*—ways of deciding.

All of these seven things must be taken into account by a communicator who wishes to send messages across cultural boundaries. They would be taken into consideration by a communicator in numbers two and three in the eight-step CIR process.

Figure 5 illustrates how these cross-cultural realities must be factored into the communication process.

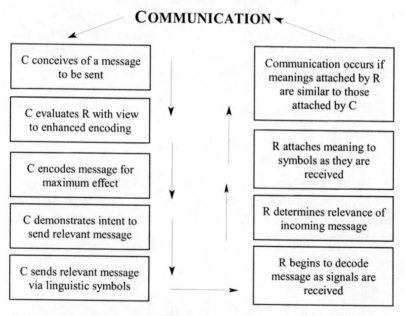

COMMUNICATION

C conceives of a message to be sent		Communication occurs if meanings attached by R are similar to those attached by C
C evaluates R with view to enhanced encoding		
C encodes message for maximum effect		R attaches meaning to symbols as they are received
C demonstrates intent to send relevant message		R determines relevance of incoming message
C sends relevant message via linguistic symbols		R begins to decode message as signals are received

FIGURE 4: THE CIR MODEL OF COMMUNICATION-ROGERS

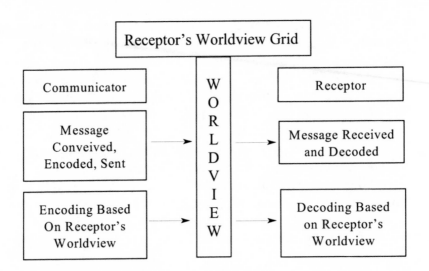

FIGURE 5: RECEPTOR ORIENTED, WORLDVIEW FOCUSED MODEL OF COMMUNICATION

This simple overview is not meant to outline the communication process in detail. It is meant to illustrate that cross-cultural communication is not a simple process and that people who are serious about missions need to take time to study cross-cultural communication.

Church (Ecclesiology)

Ecclesiological studies in the field of missiology include a study of the church proper, the history of the expansion of the church, that is, church history from a missions point of view, and the history of missions.

The Church

Missionaries need to study the church. What is the church? What is it in relation to God, to the world, to the saved, to the lost? Is there a difference between what the church is and what the church should be? These may sound like simple questions and the temptation is to offer quick and simple answers. But the relationship of God's people to him and to the world, what the church is and what it should be, what it is doing and what it should be doing, and how it should be doing it, are not easy questions to answer or problems easily solved. Missionaries must spend a great deal of time reflecting on the church: its identity, its mission, and how to more effectively be who and what God wants us to be.

Missionary Activity and The Expansion of the Church

Why is it important to study history? History is important because the present has grown out of the past. We are who we are because of who we have been. This is true of us as individuals. We are part of a genetic heritage passed from generation to generation, affecting who we are. We are also a product of our environment, past and present, affecting who we are. Experiences we have had throughout our lives combine to impact the persons we are today. If we are to understand who we are today, and why we are the way we are, we have to look to the past.

The same thing is true for a group of people. The church is a corporate entity whose present grows out of a past—two thousand years of good times and not so good times, of failures and successes, of darkness and of light. The church today is a product of its past. We are who we are because of who we have been. The only way to understand completely who we are is to understand who we have been. That is why historical studies are so important.

The history of the expansion of the church traces the spread of Christianity throughout the world from the first century to the present. A traditional approach to church history focuses on church leaders and theological developments. What questions or disputes arose? Who was involved in them? How did church leaders respond? What theology developed as a result? How did the church change over the years? What were its strong and weak points? What happened during the Patristic Period, during the Middle Ages, during the Enlightenment, the Reformation and Post-Reformation? While it is essential to have a firm grasp of church history from this point of view, for those interested in missions, it is also essential to study the spread of Christianity throughout the world during those same periods of time.

Jesus' ministry was rooted in the *missio Dei*, God's mission to reconcile lost people to himself. Jesus commissioned his followers to spread the news of the possibility of reconciliation to all people. His Jewish followers were slow to understand he meant *all* people, not just all Jewish people. For approximately ten years the church was made up of only Jewish believers. But then God helped Peter understand that *all people* meant *all* people. Soon the floodgates opened and non-Jewish believers began pouring into the church. Believers who traveled to new places, like those who arrived in Antioch (Ac. 11:19-21), told the story of Jesus to everyone who would listen. Teams of missionaries, like Paul and Barnabas, traveled to key regions and cities of the Roman Empire telling the story, establishing churches and nurturing the new believers.

Those early believers, however, were not concerned with statistics, so it is impossible to determine with any precision how many of them there were throughout the Roman world in the late first century (Hinson 1996:59). The New Testament, however, especially the book of Acts, makes it clear that Christian communities existed in major metropolitan areas as well as the smaller cities and villages of the empire. Kenneth Scott Latourette notes that, "Before A.D. 200 Christians were found not only in all of the provinces of the Empire but also outside the Empire in Mesopotamia" (1975:76). The Christian community in the city of Edessa, in the kingdom of Osrhonen, which was not incorporated into the Roman empire until A.D. 216, claimed that one of Jesus' original followers (a man named Addai, who was one of the seventy-two sent out by Jesus) established the church there (Chadwick 1993:60-61).

Though we do not know exactly when the church was established in Britain, Bishops representing the British believers attended the Council of Arles in 314 (Neill 1990:31-32). Glenn Hinson suggests that there may have been believers in Britain as early as the first century (1993:60-61). While mission outreach in Gaul (France) and Spain was slow, the story of Jesus was heartily embraced in North Africa (Neill 1990:31-34). There were believers in Arabia by the mid-third century. A mass conversion in Armenia occurred by the late third century, and by the end of the century faith communities could be found on the northern and eastern shores of the Black Sea (Latourette 1975:79-80).

The conversion of Constantine in the fourth century had a major impact on the growth of the church. Once Christianity became a protected religion, embraced by the emperor himself, being a Christian became a fashionable, politically correct choice.

A high point in the expansion of the church in the mid-fifth century was Patrick's work in Ireland. Concerning that same time frame, Robert Markus notes that there were not many pagans left in Roman towns (2001:64). By the end of the fifth century, Clovis, king of the Franks, had been converted, an event many historians consider a crucial turning point in the expansion of the faith in Europe (Neill 1990:51). Latourette notes that by the end of the fifth century there were believers in Central Asia, as well as among the Turks and Huns (1975:103).

One of the keys to the expansion and growth of the Christian faith throughout the centuries has been the rise of *renewal movements*. At various times and places the Holy Spirit has acted through individuals or groups of believers to spark a new enthusiasm for a deeper relationship with God and a new vision for what he can accomplish through those who are willing to be used in his service. Renewal movements always began and often remained on the periphery of the church, never at the center by the established leadership. Four significant renewal movements include the Waldensians, Wycliffe and the Lollards, the Dominicans, and the Franciscans.

Peter Waldo (1140-1218) became a popular preacher whose followers were sent out in teams of two. They tried to follow the Bible literally, often memorizing large portions of it, especially the New Testament. They eventually rejected the sacraments of the church, except for the Lord's Supper and baptism, for which they found biblical support. They criticized the use of Latin in worship and the strict hierarchy of the church, as well as noting the corruption that existed in the church. Their views were embraced widely in Europe and Eastern Europe and were eventually carried to America (Pearson 1998:94-100).

In the fourteenth century, John Wycliffe and his followers, known as Lollards, led a significant renewal movement. Wycliffe was an Oxford trained scholar who insisted that the Bible should be the only rule of faith in the church. He believed that church leaders who sinned, including the Pope, should be removed from office. He also rejected a number of church doctrines, including transubstantiation. He believed that preaching should be an exposition of Scripture, that the Bible should be translated into the language of the people, and that worship should be conducted in the common language (Pearson 1998:94-100).

Even though Wycliffe was denounced by the church, his influence in the English reformation was significant. The work he began in translation continues around the world today as

Wycliffe translators continue to make the Scriptures available to people in their own languages.

Dominic (1170-1222) began a renewal movement centered in the idea of preaching a message and living a life of love and service. He began with sixteen men from seven different areas of Europe who wanted to win people with the Word, not with the sword. The Dominicans (known as the Order of Preachers—O.P.) were in touch with ordinary society, focusing their significant evangelistic attention on major cities and universities where they had a major impact. While beginning on the periphery of the church, the Dominican renewal movement became more mainstream, with a Dominican Cardinal and even a Dominican Pope (Pearson 1998:94-100).

Francis (of Assisi) became the leader of another renewal movement, eventually known as the Order of Franciscan Monks (O.F.M.). While Francis was not an educated man, he was very influential, especially among working class people with little education. He took Jesus' comments about not being concerned about one's physical needs literally and espoused a life of poverty. His goal was to imitate Christ, living out the gospel without regard for material possessions, traveling about preaching the Word (Pearson 1998:94-100).

These four renewal movements, two working within the existing hierarchy of the Catholic church and two distancing themselves from the hierarchy, criticizing the abuses, illustrate how the Holy Spirit has worked over the years to raise up leaders who would point out problems or be willing to go in a different direction, allowing God to work through them to accomplish his purpose. Renewal movements have always played a crucial role in the expansion of the Christian faith.

My purpose here has not been to offer a detailed picture of the missionary expansion of the church, but to highlight the spread of the faith in the early centuries of Christianity and note the significance of renewal movements in the later centuries. The point is to understand that the spread of the

Christian faith has always been a focus for believers who understand what God wants to accomplish in his world. God has worked through his willing servants to accomplish his purpose, often raising up leaders who criticized the institutionalized church or who went about the task of missions from a new perspective. Understanding the history (who, what, when, where, why, and how) gives us a perspective on *who we have been* as God's people working with him in his world, and therefore on *who we are* working with God to accomplish his purpose in his world.

History Of Missions

Studying the history of the expansion of the Christian faith is one aspect of the historical concerns of missiological studies. The other is studying the specific ways individuals and groups have gone about the work of missions.

William Carey is considered to be the father of modern missions. In June of 1793, Carey and his family set out for India. The year before, Carey had published a small booklet entitled, *An Inquiry Into The Obligations Of Christians To Use Means For The Conversion Of The Heathens*. His point was that believers must use all the tools (means) at their disposal to tell the story of Jesus to all people. His preaching and exemplary willingness to go to distant lands stirred the hearts of people and began a movement in missions that has lasted over two hundred years.

It was not only Carey's willingness to go that led to his being held in such high regard, but the way he went about accomplishing the missionary task. Carey translated the New Testament into the local languages of the people among whom he worked, established schools, taught in a college, established a school of agriculture, established a missionary society, sent out additional missionaries, and more (George 1991). In other

72

words, William Carey utilized a multi-layered, multifaceted approach to missions that included education and other social concerns as well as direct evangelism.

William Carey represents only the beginning of a long line of dedicated people who have sacrificed a great deal in giving themselves to the Lord's service. Johannes Verkuyl, in his *Contemporary Missions* (1978—now out of print), provides a marvelous account of missions activity and studies from the sixteenth century to the middle of the twentieth century.

The importance of studying the history of missions is not rooted so much in the *who* as it is in the *how* and *why*. As noted earlier, missions involves a process of action-reflection-action. We must act, analyze our actions, looking for ways to improve, and then act again. But we do not only reflect on our own personal activity. We must reflect on the larger body of work carried on by God's people. How effective have we been? What has worked? Where has it worked? Why did it work? If something has worked in one location but not in another, why not? We must not waste time and resources repeating the mistakes of the past or engaging in ineffective methods. That is one of the primary reasons for studying history—learning from our mistakes.

Another is to see the progression of our missions outreach. How has the world changed? What kind of changes have missions undergone in response to the changes in the world? For instance, people are moving into cities faster than anyone would have imagined. How has this influx of people to major metropolitan regions affected the cities into which the people have moved, and how have those people been affected by moving there? How have these changes affected Christian missions? What are the needs of lost people who live in metropolises (cities with a population of over 100,000)? What of those who live in megacities (cities with a population of over one million)?

In 2001 there were 4,100 metropolises and 410 megacities throughout the world. According to our best statistical forecasting, by the year 2025 there will be 6,500 metropolises in the world and 650 megacities (Barrett and Johnson 2002:22-23). What do Christians working in those kinds of situations need to be willing and able to do? What methods work in those urban contexts? What does not seem to work as well? Study in the development of urban missions is essential for evangelizing a world that is rapidly becoming a world of metropolises and megacities.

If we are to do our job effectively in the future, we have to know how the job was done in the past—whether effectively or ineffectively. An awareness of our history will help us incorporate what has worked effectively and eliminate what has not.

Summary

In this chapter I have discussed the basic three-part division of missiological studies: Word, World and Church, that is, theology, anthropology, and ecclesiology.

Theology should involve investigation into hermeneutics, training in detailed textual studies, both rooted in biblical theology, which allows God to set the agenda for our theological reflection and allows us to maintain a big picture panoramic view of God's communication to us in Scripture.

Studies in cultural anthropology should include a special focus on worldviews, the deep-level unconscious assumptions on which surface-level cultural behaviors and structures are built. There must also be a focus on the process of contextualization and ethnotheologizing so local churches can be culturally appropriate rather than a fuzzy reflection of Western churches transplanted in foreign soil. Finally, there must also be inquiries into the nature of cross-cultural communication so we can make the story of Jesus relevant, meaningful and understandable to a target audience.

Ecclesiological studies, rooted in church and missions history, are important because who we are depends a great deal on who we have been. We need to learn from the past failures and past successes. We need to study how the church spread throughout the centuries. What kinds of things happened to make it possible for the story of Jesus to be told to people who had not heard it before, or to tell it in a more meaningful way to people who had heard it before but rejected it as irrelevant, insignificant, or just plain silly. We need to study the people who dedicated their lives to missions. What did they do? How did they do it? How successful were they? What worked? What didn't?

This basic three-part division of Word, World and Church is not the only way to approach the study of missiology, but it is one way that works, and makes the components of this multidisciplinary discipline easy to remember.

Chapter 4

Areas of Missiological Specialization

Beyond the basic three-part division of missiological studies: Word, World, and Church, there are also a number of areas of specialization in which missiologists can concentrate. Some of the areas of specialization are integrated in an introductory way into basic missiological studies. But selecting one or two areas of specialization will mean additional, advanced study in those areas.

In this chapter I want to highlight some of the areas of missiological concentration. I say *some* of them because it is not possible in a work of this size to create an exhaustive list of all the concentrations that may be offered at the various schools around the world that provide advanced missiological studies. The concentrations included in this chapter are representative of those offered at many of the schools offering degrees in missiology or intercultural studies.

Anthropology

Why would a missionary want to specialize in anthropology? As Kraft has pointed out:

> Anthropology is a behavioral science. . . [which attempts to] study what human beings do, how they behave. . . Anthropologists are interested in people's total behavior, not just how people think. . . This includes their work, their rituals, their child rearing,

their play, their music and art, their religion, their philosophizing, their education, their politics, their food getting, their family organization (1996:4).

Since our mission mandate is to tell the story of Jesus to every group of people on earth, it makes sense that we understand as much as we can about people in general, and specifically about the people to whom we intend to preach the gospel. Anthropology gives us the tools we need to study and understand the people to whom we will go with the good news about Jesus.

Hiebert addresses the integration of missions and anthropology, noting that:

Anthropology is of particular importance for Christian missions because missionaries are involved in building relationships and communications across cultural boundaries. Our normal response is to equate Christianity with our culture and to seek to westernize converts in other cultures. We tend to reject the practices of other cultures as unbiblical or uncivilized. Consequently Christianity is viewed by those nonwestern cultures as a foreign religion that condemns their cultural past and is irrelevant to their cultural problems. To be meaningful to people, the gospel and the church must be expressed in cultural forms that they understand and trust (1983:xx-xxi).

Anthropology is not simply a subject to be studied. The point of anthropological inquiry is to develop an anthropological, or a cross-cultural, perspective. (Kraft 1996:8). To gain this cross-cultural perspective, that is, to learn to think anthropologically, the missionary needs to study the nature of reality, perception and mental mapping. How do people *know* things? How do we perceive the world around us? How do we balance the idea of absolutes (God's absolute standards of right and wrong) with cultural perceptions of what is acceptable or unacceptable? How do we distinguish between our own cultural-bound perceptions of how things really are or how they ought to be, and God's *supracultural* perspective on how things really are or how things ought to be?

How should we think about cultures different from our own? How should we think about our own culture? What is culture? Is it a dominant force that holds us in its power, determining who and what we will be? Or is it a collectively held idea, a way of coping with life that can be adhered to or changed at will? Or is it something in between, powerful, influential, but not omnipotent or irresistible?

Where does worldview fit into culture? Are the two related? What is worldview? How does one acquire worldview? What does a person's worldview do in his or her life? Can worldview be changed? Does the Bible contain a single worldview to which all believers must adhere regardless of the culture in which they live?

What does God think about human culture? Is all human culture evil? Does God have one culture that he prefers over all others? How many different cultures can be identified in Scripture? How are cultures evaluated? How is meaning expressed in culture? What is the relationship of cultural forms to meaning? How would one go about expressing a biblical meaning in a culture which has no form similar to the biblical forms used to express the meanings you want to communicate?

These and other related issues are the kinds of things you will study in a missiological concentration in anthropology.

Contextualization

A concentration in contextualization focuses on how to

make the gospel and the church relevant and culturally appropriate in a given society. It assumes that a transplanted Western church is not what Jesus originally had in mind when he told his followers (who were not Westernized people) to go and proclaim the good news to all people. The need for contextualization grows out of an anthropologically informed view of culture and theology. It is related to anthropology, but focuses specifically on the many issues related to how one (who may be a Westernized person) tells the story of Jesus in a way that makes sense to people who have very different cultural assumptions, and practices than the person who is telling the story.

The need for contextualization is not limited only to the telling of the story of Jesus and reconciliation to God, but extends to how people live out their faith as a worshipping, serving community of God's people.

Paul wrote to the believers in Galatia about the dangers of a perverted gospel. There is just one gospel. Anyone who preaches a different gospel places himself or herself in spiritual jeopardy. But what is that one gospel? In writing to the Corinthians, Paul referred to the gospel in terms of Jesus' death, burial and resurrection. But when he preached the gospel in Pisidian Antioch (Ac. 13) it was a different presentation of the gospel than the one he preached in Athens (Ac. 17). How many ways are there to present the one true gospel? Is there a core gospel that must be proclaimed each time the story is told? If so, what is it? How does one differentiate between the cultural forms used to convey the story of Jesus as it was told in first century Jewish or Hellenistic culture and the essence of the story of Jesus that must be retold in every culture today?

Is there such a thing as an ongoing contextualized theology? Or have we, after two thousand years of Western theological reflection, arrived at the one way the truth must be explained and accepted? Is our Western theology all the theology there is? Or asked another way, is our way of thinking and reflecting about God and spiritual things the only valid way of doing so?

If theology is something to be contextualized, how do we go about doing it? What are the guidelines for contextualization? Indeed, are there guidelines? Or is culture the final standard? If absolute cultural relativity does not provide a suitable framework for life, how do we discover what absolutes exist and how do we measure culture against those absolutes? Scholars have developed a number of *models* to aid the process of contextualization. What are those models? Which one works best? Does the effectiveness of a model depend on the circumstances in which it is used, or on the presuppositions of those using the model? Or does a model's effectiveness depend on what one is trying to accomplish?

For instance, the *translation model* (of contextualization) is especially well suited for contextualizing the gospel message in the early stages of proclamation (Bevans 1992:30-46). However, in my opinion, it is not very helpful to those who may be assisting new believers in developing a culturally appropriate church in their society. What about the *anthropological model* of contextualization, the *praxis model*, the *synthetic model*, the *transcendental model*, the *critical model* or some combination of one or more of them? Which ones are most helpful in different contexts?

Obviously there is an overlap between a concentration in contextualization and one in anthropology. The ability to analyze a culture is gained from an anthropological focus. But how to bring culture and God's supracultural absolutes together to create a culturally appropriate community of worshippers requires some specialized thinking. That is the purpose behind a concentration in contextualization.

Translation

The Old Testament was written mostly in Hebrew, with a small portion of it written in Aramaic. The New Testament was written in Greek. Language is deeply tied to culture. We produce dictionaries to provide the basic or standard meanings of words. But one's cultural environment has a great deal to do with how one understands specific words. In America, for instance, when one is delighted with something or receives good news, the word *wonderful* may come to mind as an expression of delight. In Nigeria, where English is the official language, the word wonderful implies something that is amazing or difficult to understand, something that is *filled with wonder*. The idea of delight is not associated with the word wonderful in Nigeria.

The meanings we attach to words are not only connected to our cultural experience, but with our own personal experiences. For instance, a woman whose husband of forty-two years who has been incapacitated by a stroke and needed her constant attention for several years may think of different things or associate different feelings with the word *love* than a twenty-four year old man who is about to propose to the woman he *loves*. It is not a matter of the right or wrong definition of love as one might find it in a dictionary, but of the specific and personal feelings that older woman and that younger man each attach to the word *love* as they perceive it at that point in their lives. Words mean different things to different people depending on a number of factors.

The challenge of biblical translation is how to take the original message God communicated in the Scriptures and *re-communicate* it to other people so that it has the same impact on them when they hear it as the original message had on the people to whom it was first communicated. How does one go about accomplishing such a task?

Shaw has pointed out that three cultures are interacting in the translation process: the biblical culture, the culture of the translator, and the culture of the people for whom the translation is being prepared (1988:2). Discourse analysis is a tool of translation designed to help the translator understand the message of Scripture in its original historical context. What did the message mean to the people who originally received it? To understand what the message meant to the people who originally received it (including how they may have been impacted by it) the translator must understand the culture of those people—the culture of the original receptors. The translator must also understand his or her own culture and cultural assumptions so he or she can arrive at an understanding of the passage that is unencumbered (as far as humanly possible) by his or her own cultural assumptions. For example, a person educated in America in the mid to late twentieth century may simply assume that polygamy is inherently sinful. However, God never condemned polygamy. He made laws allowing it (Ex. 21:7-10), and even participated in it (2 Sam. 12:7-8) by giving David Saul's wives when David already had four of his own. Granted, polygamy was probably not what God originally had in mind as a way for men and women to interact. But how can we condemn something as inherently sinful when God himself never condemned it and even participated in it? The translator must be aware of and cautious of his or her own cultural assumptions and practices.

The concept of patriarchy provides another example of how we sometimes simply assume a thing to be right or wrong because of our cultural perspective. We assume that a patriarchal system of male dominance is what God originally had in mind for male-female interaction even though he created both male and female in his image as equals, giving each of them the same responsibility—to care for the earth. But the question is, do we find patriarchy in the Bible because God wanted it there, or because God chose Abraham and Abraham was from a patriarchal society?

Polygamy, patriarchy, and slavery along with numerous other cultural phenomena, were products of human culture that God was willing to accommodate. Understanding one's own cultural assumptions about such things is imperative for the translator if he or she is to accurately and effectively re-communicate God's message (which often includes biblical exposition) to people of other language groups.

What methodology is the translator to use in re-communicating God's message to others? Is it necessary or even possible to *literally* translate the words of the original Hebrew or Greek text into another language? What is to be re-communicated, words or ideas? How close must one stay to the original words? What is to be done if there is not a word in the receptor language that means the same thing a word meant in the Hebrew or Greek language? What if there is an idea or concept used frequently in the Hebrew Scriptures which simply does not translate into the new receptor language and culture? For instance, as noted earlier, what if the receptor culture has no knowledge of sheep or shepherding? What if the receptor culture has nothing akin to poetry in its language? The Mekeo people of Papua New Guinea have no poetry in their language. How will one translate the Psalms for them? Much of the impact of the Psalms is contained in their poetic form. To translate them as prose will fail to reproduce the impact they had when they were originally communicated. What is a translator to do?

These are the kinds of issues and questions studied by those who make translation a concentration of their missiological studies.

Leadership

Leadership as a missiological concentration has to do with developing yourself as a leader and learning how to train leaders in the context of God's global kingdom. What is leadership? Or, put another way, who is a leader? Dr. Robert Clinton has suggested that, "A Christian leader is a person with God-given capacity and God-given responsibility who is influencing a specific group of God's people toward God's purpose," (1989:7). There are not enough leaders in the church today. There are not enough effective leaders being trained in places where the church is mature, and in locations around the world where the church is young and growing fast, effective leaders cannot be trained fast enough to keep up with the spiritual needs that exist. What is to be done? We need to get busy training effective leaders.

Leadership is part of God's plan for his church. When Paul and Barnabas finished their first missionary tour, they went back to many of the churches they had established and appointed leaders in those new churches (Ac. 14:21-25). Paul sent Timothy to Ephesus to assist the leaders there and gave him instructions about appointing new leaders. Titus was left on Crete to appoint leaders in the churches there. In his letter to the churches in the area of Ephesus, Paul reminded the believers that leaders were to help the church grow and mature in the faith so the church could become a unified body of believers who knew true teaching from false teaching, and who loved one another as they went about doing the good works God had called them to do (Eph. 4:11-16).

Being a leader in the Lord's church is a great honor and a serious responsibility. Paul said it is a good thing to want to be a leader in the church (1 Tim. 3:1). But how does one become a leader? Some people are blessed with the basic skills they need to become good leaders. Others have to work hard to

85

develop the skills they need to become good leaders. Leadership training is about learning how to be a good leader, and about teaching others to be good leaders.

It is challenging to learn to be a good leader in one's own cultural context. It is challenging to teach others how to become effective leaders in one's own cultural context. Imagine the challenge of training effective leaders for cultures other than one's own. Styles of leadership which work effectively in one culture may not work at all in another. Ways of teaching leadership that work well in one culture may not work in another. Effective leadership training in a missiological context includes cultural studies so that one understands: 1) what teaching methods will work in a given culture, and 2) what leadership styles work in a given culture. Judith Lingenfelter has an article in *Missiology* (2001:XXIX (4) 449-459) about the various approaches to teaching that are successful in various cultures around the world. In *Evangelical Missions Quarterly*, James Stamoolis (2001:39 (4) 488-495) has an article in which he analyzes how the church in general is doing at training national church leaders.

Leadership training is a vital and interesting missiological concentration in which both men and women can make a significant contribution to the Lord's work around the world.

General Missiology

As the name suggests, a missiological concentration in general missiology is rooted in a broad based approach in which the student focuses his or her attention on a wide variety of issues related to missions studies and mission work. A concentration in general missiology would not necessarily include studies in each area of concentration, for there are too many of them. Instead, one may choose four or five areas of interest and take a couple of courses in each of those areas. For instance, one may choose anthropology, contextualization, theology of mission, translation and communication as areas of study. Or one may select Islamic studies, urban studies, church planting/growth, community development and leadership. Whatever combination one may choose, and whether the combination includes five areas of concentration or three, the point of a general missiology concentration is to gain as much exposure to as broad a range of missiological concerns as possible.

The value of a general missiology concentration is that if one becomes a teacher of missiology, especially at a smaller school or in a school where he or she may be the only missiological specialist, it is advantageous to have a broad foundation in the basics of missiology. Of course, the same point can be made for one going into the mission field. The broader the foundation of one's exposure to a wide range of missiological issues, the better prepared one is to deal with the many issues which will arise on the field.

This is not to say, however, that other specific concentrations are not helpful. They are. Most missionaries today go into the field as part of a team. The team will often be made up of a number of specialists. If some on the team have specialized in communication, others in anthropology and others in church planting/growth, they can combine their skills to be an effective team. Whether one specializes in a specific area or focuses on a broad range of general missiological studies is a personal choice based on the interests of the individual. Sometimes a good generalist is just what a mission team needs.

Church Planting/Growth

A concentration in church planting and church growth focuses on understanding what methods of outreach,

87

evangelism, establishing and developing churches work best in the various cultures and subcultures of the world. Obviously, what works in one culture, or even in one subculture, may not work in another. What works in a specific culture and why is the subject of inquiry in a church planting/growth concentration.

Hesselgrave has observed that, "The primary mission of the Church and, therefore, of the churches is to proclaim the gospel of Christ and gather believers into local churches where they can be built up in the faith and made effective in service, thereby planting new congregations throughout the world," (1980:20).

Hesselgrave is right. But how does one do that in a rural village in Northern Nigeria where Muslims dominate the religious landscape? How does one go about planting and building up the church in a multi-ethnic urban metropolises or megacities such as New York, Dallas/Fort Worth, or Los Angeles? The megacities of today (even those in the U.S. or Western Europe) are mission points just as much as the small village in Northern Nigeria. What are the similarities and differences in planting and building up the church in those two vastly different settings? How does one plant and build up the church among educated postmodern Westerners? How does one plant and build up the church in non-literate tribal societies? Is church planting in South America different from church planting in China? Is the task very different in societies that emphasize groupness rather than those that emphasize individuality?

If one wished to do so, it is even possible to reduce the concentration to either church planting or church growth, that is, to initially establishing the church in a specific location, or building up that church after it has been established. After all, the two tasks are very different. Each has its own specific challenges, and each has been the subject of specialized studies.

It may be that on a single mission team some of the team members specialize in the initial establishing of local churches and others specialize in building up those churches after they have been established. Or one team may be responsible for establishing churches and another may be responsible for nurturing and maturing them. The apostle Paul's mission team worked to accomplish both goals.

A concentration in church planting/growth focuses on the very heart of mission work and applies to foreign mission work as well as mission outreach right here in the U.S.

Communication

Selecting communication as a missiological concentration involves a study of how the communication process works in general, and specifically how cross-cultural communication works.

How do people communicate with one another? How do we get our meaning across to the people to whom we speak or write? Is meaning a fixed, objective reality that is simply packaged in words and sent to another person? Or is meaning more subjective, depending on the people involved in a specific communication event? Why is it that so often in the process of communication we have to stop and say, "That is not what I meant"?

What kinds of things are involved in the communication process? Is the process different if we are talking about cross-cultural communication? How does culture and worldview fit into the communication process? Does studying culture and worldview help the missionary communicate better?

Does the study of how we, as humans, communicate with each other have anything to do with how God has communicated with us in the Scriptures? Can a firm grasp of communication theory assist us in our quest for an effective hermeneutic?

Does God communicate with us the same way we communicate with each other? If we study God's communication to us using the skills and knowledge we gain from studying communication theory, will we gain new theological insights?

I believe God uses the same communication conventions to communicate with us that we use to communicate with each other. I also believe that if we study his communication to us from a communication theory perspective we will gain new insights into the message he has communicated to us. When we understand hermeneutics as a cross-cultural exercise, allowing communication theory to inform the hermeneutical process, we will be more sensitive to the way people in other cultures understand God's message as it applies to them. When we study culture and worldview we will understand the need to contextualize the re-communication of God's message so people will see the relevance of God's message for their lives.

A concentration in communication and cross-cultural communication can open new vistas of understanding and appreciation for how to study, apply, and re-communicate God's word.

Islamic Studies

Who are Muslims? What do they believe? Who was Mohammed? What is the Qur'an? Is *Allah* God? What does it mean to be Islamic? Are all Arab peoples Islamic? What is the appeal of Islam to people who are not of Arab descent? Can Muslims be converted? How? Do Muslims hate Christians? Do they hate Jews? Why are there so many problems in the Middle East? How does Abraham figure into all of this? Is Islam the fastest growing religion in the world?

There are dozens of questions like these that will be asked

and answered in a missiological concentration in Islamic Studies. The word *Islam* comes from an Arabic word that means *submission* (Saal 1991:27). Islam is a religion of submission to *Allah*, which is the Arabic word for God, the God of Abraham, the God who introduced himself to Moses as *Yahweh*.

Mohammed lived in Mecca in the sixth century. He was familiar with Jewish and Christian teaching and believed himself to be a prophet of God who was called to warn Arabs of God's anger at their idolatrous and sinful behavior, to call them to repentance and full submissive obedience to the one true God. Mohammed believed that God communicated with him directly, giving him a message in a series of visions that he repeated to his followers who memorized what Mohammed told them. Later those individuals recorded the words Mohammed spoke to them. That written record of God's message to Mohammed is called the Qur'an.

The Qur'an has much to say about *Isa*, the Arabic name for Jesus. If one studies the Qur'an and becomes knowledgeable about what it says about Isa, it is possible to lead Muslims to faith in Jesus using their own holy book. This is the approach that works best with people of Islamic faith. If one studies contextualization in conjunction with Islamic studies, he or she begins to see how it is possible for Arab people to become believers in Jesus and continue to be Arab and participate in their Muslim culture. Just as Jews can have faith in Jesus an continue to be Jewish, participating in their Jewish culture, so Arabs can have faith in Jesus (Isa) and continue to be part of a community that considers itself to be submissive to God. By remaining within the "submissive" Muslim community, Arabs who are followers of Isa, can discuss their faith in Isa with other Muslims in a way an outsider never could.

Ministering in an Islamic context can be challenging. The work is often slow and difficult. But God loves Muslims, too.

91

Jesus died for them and God wants his human children who are Muslims to come to have faith in Jesus as their savior. To work effectively among Muslims, missionaries need to learn Arabic. But to work effectively with any group of people you have to learn their language. A concentration in Islamic Studies prepares missionaries to work with one of the largest people groups on earth—people who need to learn about Jesus as God's expression of grace and mercy.

Theology Of Mission

Chuck Van Engen tells of a friend who attended a missiological conference where one of the speakers said, "There is no such thing as theology of mission or mission theology. There are only biblical exegesis, systematic theology, and mission practice. 'Mission theology' is a meaningless term, an oxymoron, for it does not refer to anything," (1996:13). With all due respect to whoever said that, he or she is quite mistaken. As I explained earlier, mission theology, or the theology of mission is reflection on how we participate with God in accomplishing his mission in the world today. It is a specific branch of theological reflection, an essential theological reflection if we are to accomplish the task Jesus has given his church.

A concentration in mission theology would include biblical and theological investigation of God's purposes and goals for his world. What has God done? How has he gone about doing it? What does he expect of his people in regard to his purposes in the world?

What did he expect of Israel? When Yahweh met his people at Mount Sinai, offering to enter into a covenant with them, he told them that if they accepted the conditions of the covenant they would become his *kingdom of priests* (Ex. 19:4-6). In ancient cultures, priests served as representatives of the god they served, representing that god to people—teaching, offering sacrifices, interceding for worshippers and so forth. The Israelites were to be an entire nation of priests representing Yahweh to the rest of the people of the ancient world. The "mission" Yahweh gave them was to proclaim him among the nations. They did this by being his holy nation, by being dedicated to him and him alone. Israel often failed to live up to God's expectations (as we often do), but mission was very much a part of God's plan during those years. Walter Kaiser has written a fine book outlining the presence of mission in the Old Testament (2000).

Just as God had missionary intentions for his people of old, he has missionary intentions for his church today. But what does it mean to be involved in missions? Is a Christian doctor who goes to distant lands to provide medical care for the poor involved in missions? Or is he or she involved in humanitarian efforts? Is mission restricted to preaching the gospel or does it include feeding the hungry? Is mission restricted to establishing churches? Or does it include establishing schools and hospitals? Jesus did not establish schools or hospitals. But he did heal people and feed people. And Paul utilized a school of sorts to preach the word in Ephesus (Ac. 19:8-10). Some might suggest that Christian missions can establish schools to teach the Scriptures, but should avoid math, science and history. These questions may seem foolish to some, but to others they are deeply held beliefs about the church's role in mission outreach. How are we to answer these kinds of questions? Should the Bible be considered as merely *descriptive*, describing what the first century church did, or is it to be understood *prescriptively*, prescribing for us (telling us) how things should be done? Inquiry into what God wants us to do and how we work with him in accomplishing his goals in the world provide the foundation for a concentration in mission theology.

Urban Missions

Urban Missions is the study of missions (needs, challenges and methods) as it relates to cities. As I mentioned earlier, in 2001 there were 4,100 metropolises (cities with a population of over 100,000) and 410 megacities (cities with a population of over one million) throughout the world. By the year 2025 there will be 6,500 metropolises in the world and 650 megacities (Barrett and Johnson 2002:22-23). The world's population is moving into its cities. Who are these people? How do they live? What kinds of needs do they have?

A quick trip through any of the world's large cities will reveal pockets of sin and suffering, poverty and despair, injustice and spiritual deprivation. What is our responsibility to the people of these cities? How should the church reach out to them? In the previous section, I raised questions related to mission theology. Are we obligated to address questions of poverty and injustice? Or does our responsibility begin and end with a proclamation of the gospel? Regardless of how you may answer that question, when it comes to proclaiming the gospel in the city, what methods work best? How do we contextualize the gospel in the city? Could it be that addressing issues of injustice, suffering, poverty, and despair are part of the contextualization process?

How, for instance, should the church work with God in the spiritual reconciliation of AIDS victims in the world's metropolises and megacities? How do we reach out to the poor, the abused, the addicted, the lonely, the marginalized? How do we reach out to the various ethnic and linguistic groups in a megacity like Los Angeles, California, which is home to people from over 140 countries speaking over 100 different languages? Multiply the numerous challenges of that reality by 410 (the current number of megacities in the world) and you begin to see the enormity of the task facing the church today.

A missiological concentration in urban studies focuses on these and other questions related to doing mission work in the world's great cities. Urban studies is the future of missions. As a larger percentage of the world's population moves into the cities over the next twenty-five years, more believers with a heart for missions in the city will be needed to meet the challenges of our new world population reality.

Community Response And Development

A concentration in community response and development assumes that believers should respond to the physical needs of a community of people. The needs can take many forms. Perhaps there is no nearby source of safe drinking water available to villagers in Northern Nigeria. The water is deep underground. Someone with the proper training and equipment needs to dig a well and train local people in the maintenance of the well and water pump. Suppose there is adequate and safe drinking water but a people's agricultural knowledge and skills (to say nothing of equipment) are lacking. Someone needs to teach them how to grow more and better food and provide them with the tools and supplies to get them started.

Suppose there has been a flood or an earthquake somewhere in Latin America and sickness is beginning to spread, to say nothing of the now homeless people who have only the clothes on their backs. How should the church respond to needs like these? What is the most effective way to help such people? Should the church leave this kind of work to the Red Cross or some government agencies so we can focus our concern on spiritual needs only? If we feel we should be involved in relief effort or community development, to what extent do we participate with other groups or agencies? What methods do we use? What are our goals? How do we balance humanitarian efforts and gospel proclamation? What if the

95

needs to which we feel we should respond are in countries where overt evangelistic proclamation is severely limited or banned altogether?

If we establish schools, hospitals or agencies of various sorts to assist local people, how many local people should be involved in the operation and maintenance and to what extent? Should the management of the agencies or institutions be turned over to local people altogether? In what kind of timeframe? Or should we retain some measure of control?

What about sociocultural issues related to the introduction of innovations into society? We in the West live in a culture that changes so rapidly that we have embraced change as a good thing. For people of traditional cultures, however, change is not always a good thing. Stories abound about simple technological advances being introduced into a society with devastating effects. The Yir Yoront people of Australia provide a classic example. When steel axes were introduced into their society, the changes that occurred nearly destroyed their society (E. Rogers 1995:412-422). We must be sure that what we do to help people really helps them rather than creating additional stresses.

Community development is important in majority world countries where the standards of living are often considerably lower than they are here in the West. However, community development is not limited to far away places and cultures. Metropolises and megacities need community response and development just as much as small rural villages. Digging wells and providing emergency or disaster relief in less technologically developed countries are important community responses. Establishing schools and hospitals in countries that are lacking in financial and technological resources are significant community development projects. But so are inner city counseling agencies, halfway houses, homeless shelters, adult education and job training facilities, and dozens of other ways of responding to the needs of people in large cities. Community response and development can be a challenging and satisfying way to participate with God in his mission in the world.

Teaching English As A Second Language

A concentration in teaching English as a second language (ESL, or TESOL, teaching English to speakers of other languages) involves two major foci: 1) learning the mechanics of teaching English as a second language, and 2) considering how one may teach English as a second language as a way to accomplish mission. Donald Snow has written a book entitled, *English Teaching As Christian Mission: An Applied Theology* (2001). His purpose is not to teach the mechanics of teaching English as a second language. Rather, his purpose is to discuss how teaching English can be mission outreach.

Snow discusses a number of important issues related to TESOL. For instance, how does the missionary balance the role of being a representative of both Christianity and of Western culture? Many people in non-Western cultures assume that Christianity and Western culture are identical. For them, embracing the West means embracing Christianity, and rejecting the West means rejecting Christianity. Obviously, the Christian English teacher does not want to leave people with that misconception. How is the misconception to be overcome? Simply explaining the difference is usually not sufficient.

In many non-English speaking countries, it is only the privileged wealthy who have an opportunity to learn English. How will teaching English to the rich in those countries fulfill one's mission calling if the Christian calling includes helping the poor and oppressed? An even more basic question has to do with how teaching English as a second language is missions as opposed to being just another way to make one's living.

Let me address the second issue first. It is important to remember that *a sermon seen is often better than a sermon heard*. People in non-Western countries where Christianity may not be part of their religious heritage, need to see how Christians live and interact with other people. A Christian living and working in a country where Christianity is not known (or at least not well known) will generate curiosity about this foreign faith. Non-Christian people will have preconceived ideas about who Christians are and how they behave. Many of their ideas will be wrong. A Christian English teacher interacting with students has an opportunity to demonstrate Christian ethics and morals, love and concern, dedication and sacrifice in a way that illustrates what Christianity is better than any sermon or Bible lesson ever could.

As for teaching only the privileged, the privileged may be those the teacher works with in his or her classes. But even English teachers do not work all the time. There is always time for Christian ministry to the poor and oppressed—even if it must be low-key and unassuming in nature.

Teaching English as a second language can be an interesting and challenging way to do the Lord's work, whether it be teaching English to immigrants here at home, or in a foreign country.

Summary

My purpose in this chapter has been to acquaint you with some of the areas of concentration available in missions studies at various Christian colleges and universities with a focus in missiology—especially at the graduate level. This is not an exhaustive list, but represents the standard offerings in missiological studies. More detailed specialization may be possible, especially at the graduate level.

The point of a concentration is to allow missionaries to customize and specialize their studies to fit their interests or needs. Missionaries must be careful, however, not to specialize too much or too soon. Some missiological programs allow students so much freedom of design that they can earn a master's degree without taking basic courses in anthropology or contextualization. That much freedom may not be a good thing. A missiologist needs a broad foundation of core courses that cover all three areas of missiological focus: Word, World and Church. Only after the broad foundation has been laid should the focus be narrowed to an area of specialization.

Part III

Mission Work

In this section, my purpose is to highlight some of the different ways one can serve in the field (Chapter 5), to discuss some basics of preparing to go into the field (Chapter 6), the importance of seeing oneself as part of a larger missiological community (Chapter 7), and finally to highlight some important missiological texts that missionaries should have as part of their growing library (Chapter 8).

Ways of Serving

My purpose in this chapter is to discuss some of the different ways people can serve the Lord in the mission field. Some of the readers of this text will already have mission experience and what I say in this chapter will not be new to those individuals. Some may be veteran missionaries, having already completed one or more full time cross-cultural mission tours. Others may have gotten their missionary feet wet by participating in a short-term mission project somewhere in the world. Some, however, may not as yet have experienced joys and challenges of the mission field. Regardless of one's level of experience, readers will probably be aware of a variety of ways they may serve as missionaries. My goal is not so much to provide new information on ways missionaries can serve, but to discuss some of the standard options in light of a basic introduction to missions and missions training.

Long-term Service

It is essential that the church recognize and stress the need for full-time, long-term (two years or more) missionary service. Under the right circumstances (which includes pre-field training, careful selection of field location, and proper supervision) short-term missions can serve a useful purpose. But no amount of short-term missions can take the place of full-time, long-term mission service. Incarnational ministry, which includes learning the culture and language of a people, gaining their trust so that you can work effectively among them, learning how to contextualize the gospel and to help new believers develop a contextualized theology takes time—sometimes a long time. Doing the job effectively requires a long-term commitment. Addressing the need for renewal in long-term mission commitments Robert Coote notes that:

> In a world where hundreds of millions have yet to hear the name of Christ and additional millions have not yet heard the Gospel presented *effectively* in their cultural context, there is no substitute for the career missionary. Making this assumption, one can take only limited satisfaction in reports of uncounted thousands of short-termers engaged in mission, of local churches and schools undertaking cross-cultural "exposure" forays, and of various forms of high-tech media lending support to the proclamation of the Gospel. These and other positive factors cannot balance a real decline in long-term commitments by men and women who are prepared to take a profoundly incarnational approach to communicating the Gospel of Jesus Christ to people of other cultures (1995:6)

Again, this is not to detract from the value of short-term missions. But short-term mission service cannot replace long-term service. Some things can be accomplished in the short term. Others cannot. And much of what cannot be accomplished in the short term lies at the very heart of missions. Effective missions outreach is incarnational. Missions needs to be viewed from a long range, incarnational perspective.

Pioneer Work

The term *pioneer work* refers to mission outreach among *unreached* or *unchurched* (also referred to as least reached) people groups, meaning specific sociolinguistic groups of people where there is little or no evangelistic presence. Fortunately, there are fewer and fewer people groups that have not had at least some exposure to the gospel. However, significant numbers of people still fit into this category.

Missiologists classify *"least reached"* people groups as groups where less than 50% of the people have heard the gospel. Most of these people groups live in what is referred to as the *10/40 window*, which is the "rectangular-shaped window 10 degrees by 40 degrees north of the equator spanning the globe from West Africa to Asia, including over 60 countries and more than 2 billion people" (Love 2000:938).

Sub-Saharan Africa is an example of a region of the world in the 10/40 window that includes a number of least reached groups of people. Johnstone and Mandryk list eleven groups of people in this region as fitting into this least reached category: "Malinke, Soninke, Fulbe, Wolof, Gur, Chadian peoples, Hausa, Songhai, Kanuri, Zerma, Pygmy," (2001:16).

Mission work among groups like these can be a difficult but rewarding experience. It is often slow, for it takes time to understand a people and gain their confidence. This kind of work should only be considered from a long-term perspective. There may not be as many unreached people as there used to be, but teams of well-trained, committed missionaries are still needed to do pioneer work among the unreached peoples of the earth.

Church Planting

The term *church planting* generally refers to the work of

evangelizing people and establishing new churches in geographic regions (or among a specific people group within a geographic region that may be inhabited by multiple sociocultural groups) where the church already has an established presence. Missionaries involved in church planting follow those engaged in pioneer work, continuing and expanding the outreach of the pioneers, establishing new churches in villages, communities or neighborhoods.

There are a number of methods or models that can be used to plant churches. Craig Ott discusses three models of church planting (2001:338-344): *pastoral, apostolic, catalytic*.

According to Ott, *pastoral* church planting involves establishing a new church and pastoring it until the church can call and support its own pastor, at which time the missionary can move on to another location and establish another church. The model is simple. After initial evangelistic efforts have produced a small group, the missionary usually finds it necessary to shift from an emphasis on outreach to one of nurturing, providing the spiritual care the new group needs until one or more of them is mature enough to provide that care.

Because of its simplicity, and because most students trained in ministry are trained to work from a pastoral point of view, the pastoral model of church planting is often used without the benefit of critical analysis to determine whether or not it is the most effective model in a given location. It may be. But it may also not be the most effective model.

The second of the three models Ott discusses is the *apostolic* model. Here the missionary models himself or herself after the apostle Paul. Paul's method of ministry did not include a lot of localized pastoral work. Paul preached the gospel and taught new believers enough of the truth for them, along with the help of the Holy Spirit, to be able to function without his (Paul's) continued presence. He empowered the local people to lead and expected them to be responsible for helping other, newer believers. Occasionally, Paul would send one or more of his mission team back to a church he was especially concerned about so they could provide additional pastoring support. But even that was usually short-term. Paul's expectation was clearly that local people, depending on the Holy Spirit for insight and understanding, would be able to provide the leadership the new church needed. Sometimes he had to write to them, expressing concerns, exhorting and encouraging them. But Paul did not consider it his responsibility to settle down in one place and pastor a church. He was a church planter, teaching and empowering local people to look to the Holy Spirit for the help they needed in seeing to their own spiritual needs.

The apostolic model of church planting approaches the task in a similar manner. Missionaries evangelize people and establish churches. They spend enough time with the new believers to help them understand the basics, which includes developing an awareness and dependence on the Holy Spirit. As people are saved and begin worshipping together, the new believers are expected to participate in and lead in worship, Bible study, and, as appropriate, engage in pastoring responsibilities. The missionary does not preach. He or she does not lead, does not make decisions, does not say, "This is the way we did it back home." The missionary acts as a consultant, asking rather than answering questions. Instead of providing direct answers questions like, "How are we supposed to do this?" (thus structuring the church in Western ways) the missionary may say, "I'm not sure. In your own culture, how would you do something like this?" Using the critical model of contextualization, the missionary will help the people develop a contextualized theology and worship.

Before long the new church and the missionary are ready to begin the separation process. Perhaps he will be gone for one Sunday, scouting out opportunities in another nearby location. Soon he or she will be gone from there more than he or she is present and can eventually leave the new church to function on its own. This is what Paul did and it is an effective model for church planting.

The third model Ott highlights in his article is the *catalytic* model. The catalytic model is similar to the apostolic model in that the missionary does not function as a pastor. Instead he or she serves as a consultant and facilitator, encouraging new believers to select, train and send one of their number to another location to plant a new church. The missionary does the same kinds of things in the catalytic model he or she does in the apostolic model, except instead of the missionary going to plant a new church, one of the new believers goes. This allows the new church to participate fully at a very young age in Jesus' plan for his people and his churches to share the message of hope with those who, as of yet, have no hope.

There are other models of church planting that may be similar to these or which may involve aspects of each of these. There is no one model that is best. The point in planting churches is to analyze a cultural situation and do what will work best in that culture. I have highlighted these three to give you an idea of the kinds of issues that face those who choose planting churches as their way of serving our Lord.

Teaching

Another way to serve as a missionary is to be a teacher. Though there are numerous ways one can serve as a teacher, I want to highlight two in this section: teaching Bible and ministry in a Bible college or seminary in a foreign field, and teaching English as a second language. I will have more to say about teaching and education in general in a later section.

Teaching Bible, Ministry And Missions

Even when we prepare for cross-cultural service, even when we practice incarnational missions and ministry, even when we spend years of service in a given cultural setting, gaining the trust and confidence of the local people among whom we work, we must still realize that we can never be as effective working among the general population of that culture as one who is a native of that culture. A cultural outsider can never work as effectively with a group of people as can a cultural insider. That being the case, the most effective outreach and ministry in any culture can (and must) be done by local people. It makes sense, then, to spend time (and money and effort) training local men and women to serve the national church. They can do a better job of serving their people than we can.

There are two important questions to be considered when thinking about how to educate local believers to serve the local church: 1) can a college or seminary do the job better than the local church, and, 2) if in any given area it is decided that a college or seminary is the appropriate way for people to be trained for leadership in the local church, are they being trained (either consciously or unconsciously) to duplicate the Western church or are they being trained to develop a truly contextualized local church?

It may be that in a given area, depending on how the people of that culture are normally trained and educated in life, that the local church itself is the best option for training leaders for the local church. In a culture where people grow up learning by doing as they work alongside parents and other "teachers" that the best thing for a church to do is to continue that educational tradition and train church leaders using that same process. This is the way Jesus trained his followers. The apostles were not sent off to a formal school where they learned how to be apostles. They traveled around with Jesus, watching, listening, doing as they were given opportunity and assignment. It was (and continues to be) an effective way to train church leaders.

However, a college or seminary may also be an appropriate way to train church leaders depending on how long the church has been established in that region, and what training and educational traditions work effectively in that culture. If a college or seminary is an appropriate way to train church leaders in a given culture, individuals who are qualified to teach Bible and ministry at a college level are important members of the larger missionary community.

The word *qualified* becomes a crucial consideration in the larger question of the kind of training being offered. When I say *qualified* I am not referring to qualifications related to Bible and ministry as they might be taught in a Western college or seminary. An individual who, by virtue of training and degrees earned, is qualified to teach in a college or seminary here in the West, will also be academically qualified to teach in a college or seminary in another culture. Academic competency in one's field, be it Bible, ministry or whatever, is not the issue. When I speak of being *qualified* to teach in a cross-cultural context, I am referring to being trained as a cross-cultural missionary, capable of suspending one's Western assumptions and worldview (as much as is humanly possible), teaching Bible and ministry in a contextualized way.

Those who train church leaders in foreign cultures must not make the mistake of training them in Western ways of thinking and doing. The teacher's job is not to create Western church leaders in non-Western cultures. The teacher's job is to help students understand the historical context of the Scriptures and then help them to apply what they learn to their own native culture—which will be different from the cultures represented in the Scriptures and different from the home culture of the

110

teacher. As in the translation process, the missionary Bible teacher is dealing with three different cultural settings: 1) the cultures represented in the Scriptures, 2) his or her own culture (usually Western), and 3) the culture of the people with whom he or she is working. The teacher must understand all three cultures and keep the distinctions between them clearly in mind as he or she explains the historical context and helps local believers apply the Scriptures to their own cultural context.

The teacher must avoid the temptation to suggest ways to apply the Scriptures. A better approach is to explain what Jesus and the early believers did and then ask students what would be an appropriate way to accomplish the same thing in their culture. A good cross-cultural teacher asks more questions than he or she will answer.

Whatever approach one uses to teach Bible and ministry, the point is not to duplicate the Western church in non-Western cultures, but to assist students in developing a contextualized local church.

When it comes to teaching missions to national church leaders the key is to help them avoid the mistake Western missionaries so often make: *assuming that the way we do things back home is the way these new believers in this new place should do them as well.* National church leaders and perspective missionaries need to study culture and contextualization just as much as Western missionaries do.

Many people are surprised to learn that there are as many (if not more) non-Western cross-cultural missionaries working throughout the world than there are Western missionaries. New believers around the world have taken seriously their responsibility to share the gospel with the lost. They are just as willing, if not more willing, than many Western believers to share their faith with people of other cultures. But just as Western missionaries, they are inclined to think that the way they do things is the best way to do things. They are just as likely to import their culturally-impacted way of "doing Christianity" as are Western Christians. When we teach new believers about the need to carry the gospel to all the world, we also need to teach them about the need to contextualize it. Of course it will be difficult and embarrassing for us to teach them about contextualization if we have not practiced it ourselves.

Teaching English As A Second Language

Some cultures in the world hold America and the West in general in very high esteem. But many do not. Many countries are anti-Western and anti-Christian. They do not want Christians coming into their country trying to convert their people to what they consider to be a foreign, Western religion. Many non-Western nations of the world consider Christianity and the capitalistic West (which means the greedy, decadent, immoral West) to be one and the same. What this means in practical terms is that many countries are not open to Christian missionaries. If you apply for a visa listing *missionary* as your occupation or as the reason for coming to their country, you will be denied.

There are still over 1.6 billion people in the world who are *unevangelized* (Barrett and Johnson 2002:22-23). Unevangelized does not mean people who are not Christians. It means people among whom there is little or no evangelism being done. 1.6 billion. That's a lot of people who have no opportunity to hear the gospel. Most of them live in countries where Christian missionaries are not welcome. The problem is obvious. What is the solution? One way to gain entry into countries otherwise closed to Christian outreach is to go into that country as an English teacher.

Even countries not sympathetic to Western values and perspectives realize the importance of speaking English, for much of the world's commerce is conducted in English. Since

112

native English speakers (such as Americans) can teach English better than a local person for whom English is a second language, Americans can gain access into countries as English teachers when, as missionaries, they would be rejected.

Teaching English as a form of mission in cultures that are not fully appreciative of Western values and which are not open to Christian witness can be slow and frustrating work. English teachers must be careful not to violate working agreements regarding Christian witness. Circumstances may vary from country to country. It may be that in some countries teachers are not allowed to initiate conversations about their Christian faith, but if asked, may explain what they believe and why. But what if students do not ask? In some of the more oppressive countries, students are warned not to become friendly with their English teacher. They are in class to learn English, not to make friends with an American. That can be frustrating for the teacher. His or her reason for being there is to connect with people and witness to them. If you can't connect, you can't witness. The work is often slow and frustrating. But as Donald Snow points out, one way to deal with the frustration is to view Christian service as a form of mission (2001:16).

Being in a foreign culture as a teacher of English, living and working as a Christian in a society where there are not many believers, is a form of mission. Think of the advice Peter gave women believers who were married to men who were not believers. Peter explained that the life one lives is a powerful form of Christian witness (1 Pet. 3:1-2).

Before his death, Bishop Stephen Neill used to tell of a Christian woman (a British missionary) living in a Muslim country. Opportunities to witness were few. One day the woman had gone to buy some flowers for her daughter's birthday. On the way home from the market, a Muslim woman standing in the door of her house saw the British woman

113

walking by with the flowers and remarked how beautiful they were. The British woman said, "They are lovely, aren't they? I just bought them for my daughter's birthday. But if you would like them I would be happy for you to have them. I know my daughter would not mind if I gave them to you." The Muslim woman was surprised and wanted to know why the British woman would do such a thing. The British woman was then able to explain that as a Christian she was happy to be able do something that made others happy. As a result of that encounter, a number of Muslim women on that street heard about Jesus. In many cases, the opportunities are few, but for those who see the Christian life itself (a life of service and kindness) as a form of witness, teaching English in a culture that would otherwise be closed to Christian witness can be a rewarding form of service.

Not all situations where one could serve as an English teacher would be so restrictive. In some countries, the official policy may not allow missionaries into the country. However, once one has entered the country to teach English or offer some other service, Christian witness is welcome. Many missionaries are serving happily with many opportunities for witnessing and teaching because of the contacts they make as English teachers. Many of them even use a simple English translation of the Bible as their main textbook.

There are a number of programs in Christian colleges and seminaries designed to prepare individuals academically to teach English as a second language as a form of Christian missionary service.

Bible Translation

There are roughly 6,000 language groups in the world. The Scriptures (or some portion of them) have been translated into about half of them. It is wonderful that at least some of

God's word is available in nearly half of the languages of the world. But what of the remaining language groups—nearly 3,000 of them? At present, a new translation project is begun about every two weeks. At that rate it will be many life times before God's word is available in every human language. The Wycliffe Bible Translators has set a new goal. By the year 2025 they want to have a translation project under way for each of the remaining language groups which do not yet have their own translation of the Scriptures. For that goal to be realized, two or more new translation projects will have to be started each week for the next 24 years.

In the past, an individual with linguistic and theological training would live among a group of people who did not have the Scriptures available to them in their mother tongue, or as it is also called, their *heart language*. The translator would learn their language and then begin the slow, tedious process of translating the Scriptures into the language of the people. In recent years however, it has become apparent that local believers who already know their language can communicate (i.e., re-communicate) God's word in their language more effectively than can someone who has only recently learned their language. Bible translation organizations now make use of local believers (called mother tongue translators, MTTs) working as part of a translation team to produce accurate, understandable (and therefore relevant) translations of God's word (Shaw 2000:123-126).

Missionaries who want to work as Bible translators can receive training in translation theory and work as consultants in the translation process, assisting local translation teams, often headed by a local missionary. A translation consultant may travel to several different locations each year, participating in local translation projects. His or her participation may include answering questions related to the Greek or Hebrew text, the biblical culture involved in a specific text, translation options, doctrinal issues, decisions regarding idiomatic expressions, or a number of other questions which may arise in the process of completing a translation of God's word into a local language.

Or, instead of being a consultant, traveling to different locations, a missionary, after being trained in translation theory, may choose to concentrate his or her efforts in one location for an extended period of time, acting as the team leader for a translation project which utilizes the talents and skills of MTTs.

Either way, serving as a Bible translator has always been a crucial part of the church's larger mission outreach. When a group of people have the Scriptures available to them in their own heart language God is able to speak to their hearts in a way that is not possible if they have to rely on a translation of a second or a trade language.

Medical Missions

Medical missions is not a new idea. John Thomas worked with William Carey in India in the late 1700's to improve the quality of life and health for the Indian people (Campbell 2000:611-613). Originally the term medical missions applied to work done in direct relation to a hospital or clinic. More recently, however, the term has been broadened to include not only primary health care, but also preventive medicine and community issues such as clean water, adequate sanitation, immunization, nutrition, general health care concerns, and education. Obviously, one does not have to be a medical doctor to be involved in medical missions.

There will always be a need for doctors, physician assistants (PAs), and nurses in the foreign mission field. But individuals with degrees in public health, or health care technicians of various kinds (vision or dental, for example), and medical assistants who can assist doctors are also needed in missions endeavors. So are hospital and clinic administrators, and people who can maintain the facilities and equipment. Since medical missions also includes things like clean water and adequate sanitation, people with the skill to dig wells and construct sanitation facilities are also essential. In addition to building, maintaining, staffing and operating stationary medical facilities, there is also the challenge of the logistics involved in mobile health care facilities. When people and delicate equipment have to be moved, often over rough terrain, someone has to plan and supervise such movement.

Even if you are not a doctor or a nurse, you can still be involved in medical missions, for medical missions is a multifaceted endeavor requiring expertise in any number of fields.

Urban Missions

Urban missions has to do with outreach and Christian service in the city. As noted earlier, the future of missions is in the metropolises and megacities of the world. Cities are growing faster than anyone imagined they would. By mid-2002, 133,600 people moved into cities somewhere in the world each day—not each year, or month or week, but *each day* (Barrett and Johnson 2002: 22-23). At present there are still more people in rural areas than in urban settings, but not many. Over the next twenty years that reality will change dramatically. More people will live in cities than will live in rural areas. At present, just under 3 billion of the world's 6 billion people live in cities. Less than 2 billion of them are believers. That means that over 1 billion of the people living in the world's cities are not Christians. Many of those lost people are also marginalized, alone, abused, addicted, afraid, oppressed, homeless, ill or suffering in some other way. What is to be done? What would Jesus do? Jesus would be among those people, compassionately serving them just as he was among the poor and outcast of his day.

My focus in this section is not so much on what kind of mission service one does (church planting, teaching, translation), but on where one does it. The basic categories of mission service in which one can engage in a rural setting (in an African or Indian village for example) can also be accomplished in an urban setting, a Western or non-Western metropolis or megacity.

Western Urban Missions

We usually think of missionaries as people who go off to far away places, often exotic and sometimes isolated. But since God's mission in the world is to reconcile lost people to himself, restoring them to a healthy relationship with himself, anytime and anywhere we are working with God to accomplish that purpose, we are missionaries. Far away or nearby, missions is still missions.

Big cities, whether metropolises or megacities, take on a life and identity of their own. Each has a personality that is unique to it. New York is very different from Los Angeles. Each has its own unique look and feel, its own community idiosyncrasies. Chicago and Miami are as different from each other as each of them is different from New York and Los Angeles. London, Paris and Vienna, which are also Western cities, are also unique with their own distinct personalities. But all big cities also have certain things in common. They are all multi-ethnic and all have large populations of people who do not yet know the Lord, many of whom are in need of a compassionate friend to extend a hand and lead them into a relationship with their savior.

How does one go about meeting the needs of the unsaved

in large Western cities? In the space permitted, I can mention only a few possibilities.

In any large Western city there will already be groups of believers worshiping and serving God. Many of them will already be of substantial size and may already be involved in some form of outreach into some portion of their community. However, their may be a specific group of people (one of the many sociolinguistic subcultures) among whom there is no specific evangelistic effort. For instance, there are over 100 different language groups represented in Los Angeles—some statistics suggest over 130. It may be that several of those groups have no Christians working among them, contextualizing the gospel to their needs. In every urban context, missionary teams need to target those ethnic groups and begin working with them.

Another approach to Western urban missions is a focus on those who are suffering: the homeless, abused, addicted, or those who are in some way marginalized or forgotten. Shelters that provide a safe, dry, warm place to sleep and a hot meal, agencies that provide counseling, half-way houses that help people transition back into a productive life: these and a dozen other ways to help people allow Christians to demonstrate God's love and concern for people in need. They provide an avenue for *living witness* as well as opportunities to witness directly as we interact with the people being served.

Not all believers are convinced of the need for this kind of *holistic mission*, the goal of which is to minister to the needs of the whole person. I wonder sometime if we haven't overlooked the point of Jesus' parable of the Good Samaritan. In the story, as Jesus told it, no preaching, teaching or witnessing occurred. It was about a man who saw another human being in need and did something to help him. (I will have more to say about the Good Samaritan in the next section.) I am not suggesting that we need not speak up and try to win people to Jesus. Of course

119

we should do that. But we should not forget the power of the good deed, the helping hand, the kind word of love and encouragement. Building a relationship with people in need may make it possible for us to lead them into a relationship with God—which is exactly what missionaries are supposed to be doing.

Non-Western Urban Missions

Many of the same kinds of things that can be done in large Western cities can be done in non-Western urban settings as well. In many respects urban missions, Western or non-Western, are similar. They both involve large groups of people living in close proximity to each other, some rich, some poor, some powerful, some not. Most of them will not know the Lord. Teams of believers need to work among them, identifying and meeting their needs, leading them into a relationship with the Lord. But in some ways non-Western urban mission will be quite different from Western urban missions. For instance, an American mission team working in Los Angeles may be able to set up agencies and offer assistance coordinated with other agencies in a way that may not be possible in a non-Western setting.

The differences that must be taken into account exist not only between Western and non-Western cities, but between non-Western cities in different regions of the world. For instance, urban missions in Lagos, Nigeria, a city with a diverse population of many millions, will be very different from urban missions in Moscow, Russia, also a diversely populated non-Western megacity. African people and Russian people have very different worldviews and cultures. Therefore, they have different needs, different ways of responding, especially in areas of spiritual matters and must be approached differently with a different set of expectations regarding their response.

The two things I want to emphasize in this section on urban missions are: 1) the importance of a focus on urban missions, and 2) the need for additional Western urban missions. In the not too distance future, most of the people on earth will live in cities. We need to adjust our missions focus to urban missions. And while many of the world metropolises and megacities will be in majority world countries (i.e., non-Western countries), we cannot forget about the lost right here in our own part of the world. "Go" does not always require going half way around the world to another country. "Go" can also mean going from Texas to Los Angeles, or from Indiana to New York, or to Chicago, San Francisco, New Orleans, Miami, Seattle, or Washington D.C. People from all over the world come to America looking for a better life. We need to see to it that they do truly have a chance to enjoy the abundant life Jesus has to offer.

Community Relief And Development

In this section I want to suggest some basic ideas related to community relief and development. There is far too much to discuss to cover the material in any depth, but key points deserve at least some basic discussion.

I have made it clear in previous sections that Christian mission involves Christian service. I also want to make it clear, however, that I do not support the position that Christians should make Christian service an end in itself. God's mission in the world is to save the lost. Therefore our mission, as his representatives in the world, working with him to accomplish his purpose, is also to save the lost. But sometimes the best way to save the lost is to serve their physical needs without trying to convert them right there on the spot.

In the previous section, I made reference to Jesus' story of the Good Samaritan. I pointed out that in the story there was no mention of preaching or teaching. Of course, the man the

Samaritan was helping was a Jew, already in covenant relationship with God. What would the Samaritan's verbal witness have been about? The absence of verbal witness, however, does not eliminate witness. The Samaritan man's actions were a powerful witness to his appreciation of humanity, even for a Jew who probably hated him and would not have stopped to help him if the circumstance had been reversed. The Samaritan's actions also spoke of his understanding of the need to do good to others, and perhaps even to his insight into God and his desire for all people to love one another. The Samaritan man may not have spoken with his mouth, but he did speak. And Jesus commended him for his actions.

My point is that we need to strike a balance. Our primary goal must be reconciliation and relationship. God's goal must be our goal. How do we accomplish that goal? We must remember that not only have we been given the *Great Commission*, to go and preach, but also the *Great Command*, to love our neighbor as we love ourselves. Perhaps it is in the combination of the two that we accomplish the greatest good for God.

Having said that, let me proceed to a brief discussion of how we can accomplish the Great Commission and the Great Command by helping people in need.

Disaster Relief

Jesus said there would always be wars, earthquakes and famines. He didn't mention fires, tornadoes, hurricanes, mud slides, tidal waves, volcanoes or other natural disasters. Whether Jesus mentioned them or not is hardly the point. Wherever there is a disaster and people are suffering because of it, God's people should be there, offering assistance and support.

Disaster relief involves two basic issues: funding and

distribution. Someone has to raise the funds to support the relief efforts, and someone has to oversee the distribution of the supplies to be distributed. The "supplies" may be food (including clean water), clothing, medical supplies (and the people to administer them), tools and material for rebuilding, seed for planting, or other essentials to help people survive and recover from disaster. Whatever they are, they are going to cost money. Where will the money come from? Someone needs to raise it. Fundraising is an essential aspect of mission work. As funds are received and goods purchased to be distributed to those in need, someone has to be on site at the location of the disaster to oversee the distribution of the goods. Both jobs (fundraising and distribution) are essential to disaster relief.

It is very difficult for one person to be involved effectively in both fundraising and distribution. Fundraising normally takes place in the States, while distribution is usually in another part of the world. However, it is important for fundraisers to visit disaster sites as often as possible so he or she can explain and discuss the needs from a personal perspective. It is also important for those who oversee the distribution of goods to make visits to supporters, relating stories and first-hand accounts of the needs and how the donated goods are making a difference in people's lives.

Disaster relief is an important subcategory of community development. It can provide the foundation for long-term development projects. It can be expensive, but most worthwhile project usually are.

Education

In a previous section I discussed the importance of teaching Bible and ministry so local people can be trained for effective ministry. Here I am discussing education in general.

123

There can be serious problems associated with the introduction of Western-style formal education into cultures where formal classroom instruction has not been an integral part of their social system. Its introduction has proven disruptive in some cultures, separating children from their parents for several hours each day, interrupting the traditional educational process, including the transmission of important cultural information and behaviors that had normally been communicated over the course of day-to-day interaction between parents and children. Missionaries working in traditional cultures should exercise special caution in introducing practices that can disrupt the normal traditional educational process.

To the Western missionary it may appear that many traditional societies do not have an educational system. A society may not have a *formal Western* kind of a system, but they do have a system. Because their educational system does not look like and function like ours does not mean that they do not have one. As children participate with their parents and extended family members in daily activities they are learning what they need to learn to function in their society. They are being educated. Disrupting that educational process with the implementation of different system that has a different goal and a different focus (perhaps reading and writing) runs the risk of disrupting culture at both the immediate family level and at the larger community level.

However, having acknowledged the dangers of implementing formal education in a traditional society, it must also be noted that due to globalization the world is becoming a much smaller place. Even traditional societies feel the increasing influence of Western thinking and technology. Many people from traditional societies recognize the need (especially for their children) to be able to function in a world that extends far beyond their immediate cultural context. Many of them welcome a Western style formal education as an addition to their traditional education. With a sensitive awareness of the importance of combining the two kinds of education (traditional and Western) an effective middle ground can be reached.

What is the goal of education as it falls under the umbrella of community development? From that point of view, the goal is to educate people in areas that can improve their health and living conditions. These might include health and hygiene classes for women, and classes on farming techniques designed to produce higher crop yields for men. Basic literacy classes are also important for further development.

Those kinds of efforts are designed for more immediate results in the adult community. Providing children with a Western style education looks to the future, giving children the chance to have very different lives than their parents could ever hope to enjoy. Of course, many traditional peoples are happy with their lifestyle and do not want a different life. Should that decision not be respected?

Primary and Secondary Schools

If a Western style formal education is going to be made available to the children of a non-Western culture, what should the goals of that education be? The first goal should be to affirm the value of their traditional society. They need to feel good about who they are, not embarrassed because they are not Americans. Becoming literate and able to function in a technologically advanced world does not mean becoming an American. It does not mean thinking, looking or acting like an American.

The second goal should be to give the child what he or she needs to function in the larger world, the world beyond his or her immediate sociocultural context. The third goal (and for the missionary/teacher perhaps the most important goal) is imparting Christian values. This goal must be closely associated with the first goal, affirming their traditional culture. Christian values are not *American* Christian values. One of the most difficult tasks missionaries have is separating their Western view of things from a purely Christian view of things.

Many of the values we hold dear as Christians are cultural values that reflect the way we, as Western believers, live out our faith. People in other cultures may have different views than we do about whether or not a particular behavior is Christian. For instance, in Western culture it is essential that a woman conceal her breasts. In many other cultures it is not. In some Middle Eastern cultures women who go out in public must be completely covered head to toe in order to be modest. Do our standards of modesty represent the essential and correct standards of modesty for every culture, or are our standards culturally determined standards? In order to impart Christian values to students, but not *Western* Christian values, missionaries need to know the difference between the two.

Trade and Technical Schools

Beyond the primary and secondary school levels, missionaries can provide valuable community development in the form of trade and technical school training. In most majority world countries, the family farm is a basic reality. But seldom does it provide sufficiently for all the needs of the family. Learning a trade or gaining a technical skill can make an important difference in an individual's ability to provide for his or her family. Trades and technical skills which may be useful include gaining proficiency as a photographer, a tailor, a printer, a mechanic, plumber, electrician, in shoe repair, carpentry, basic office skills (typing, photocopying, filing, record keeping), in business bookkeeping, masonry, and any other trade or technical fields one can name.

One school I know of in Jos, Nigeria, holds classes in ministry training and biblical studies in the mornings and technical and trade training classes in the afternoon. When students graduate and leave to become church leaders, in addition to their biblical studies and ministry skills they also have a technical or trade skill with which they can support themselves.

Parachurch Agencies

Examples of parachurch agencies include orphanages, shelters for the homeless or victims of abuse, or counseling centers serving the needs of individuals suffering from addiction. The need for specific kinds of agencies will differ from culture to culture. For instance, in many majority world countries there is a tremendous need for orphanages. There may be little need however, for counseling centers for victims of addiction in those same cultures. The needs of the people in a given geographic region will determine what kind of parachurch agencies are appropriate.

Orphanages

James explained that the kind of religion (or expression of faith) that interests God is one that includes caring for widows and orphans (Jas. 1:27). In some cultures, individuals without the benefit of an extended family to care for them are extremely vulnerable. This is especially true of children. There are many regions in the world where the ravages of war or epidemic have left children without parents or other family members to care for them. The AIDS epidemic (especially in Africa) is an example. By the end of the year 2000, 13 million children (90% of whom live in Africa) were orphans because of AIDS.

Most of them were under the age of fifteen. The U.S Agency for International Development suggests that by the year 2010, nineteen sub-Saharan [African] countries will have a combined total of 40 million orphans, largely due to AIDS. The worldwide total by 2010 will reach 100 million (Action For Orphans 2000).

Governments in these regions usually lack the resources to offer meaningful assistance. If assistance is to be offered it must come from humanitarian agencies. Since God expects his people to be involved in this kind of work, mission agencies should place the care of orphans high on their list of priorities.

In some locations, adequate facilities will be available. Funds and people to manage and staff the facilities are the primary needs. In other locations, adequate facilities do not already exist and land must be acquired (via purchase, lease, grant or gift) and facilities built. Someone has to design and oversee the building of the facilities. In those cases, architects, contractors and builders, who may not otherwise think of themselves as "missionaries," become an intricate and invaluable part of a mission team whose "outreach" will be expressing their faith and God's love and concern by helping the helpless.

Tens of millions of children throughout the world are orphans. What better way to teach them about God's love for them than by loving them and caring for their needs?

Homeless Shelters

As I have said previously, we tend to think of missions as being "over there, far away." Some of it is. But wherever there are people in need, God's people need to be busy meeting those needs. In America in 1988, 500,000 to 600,000 people were homeless. When space was available they slept in homeless shelters, ate in soup kitchens. Usually they gathered on the streets. By 1999 the numbers had risen to 700,000 people being homeless on any given night, with 2 million people over the course of the year experiencing some level of homelessness (National Coalition for the Homeless 1999:Fact Sheet #2).

While it is impossible to measure homelessness with complete accuracy, it is clear that more people in America are homeless than had been previously imagined. There are many reasons for homelessness. Some are more easily addressed than others. For some, homelessness is temporary. For others it is a more permanent situation. Regardless of the reasons for homelessness, huge numbers of people loved by God—people who are created in his image—are cold, hungry and homeless. Just as orphanages provided by Christians provide an atmosphere of love and an expression of God's concern for children without parents, homeless shelters provided by Christians provide an atmosphere of love and an expression of God's concern for people who are cold, hungry and without a place to call home. Providing shelter for the homeless (regardless of why they are homeless) is a way of carrying out the *Great Commandment* portion of God's purpose in the world.

Centers For Victims Of Abuse And Addictions

Beyond orphanages and homeless shelters, another way to serve hurting and often helpless people is through assistance centers, including counseling centers emergency shelters, halfway houses and rehabilitation centers, for helping victims of child and domestic abuse, and drug or alcohol addiction.

Police spend approximately one third of their time responding to calls related to domestic violence. Six million American women are beaten each year by their husbands or boyfriends. Four thousand of them die. Sixty-four percent of all women are battered at some point in their lives. Sixty percent of those women are pregnant when the assault occurs. FBI statistics indicate that every twelve seconds a woman is physically assaulted by her husband or boyfriend (Women's Coalition of St. Croix 2002).

In studies completed between 1986 and 1997, incidents of the various kinds of child abuse (physical, sexual, emotional) increased anywhere from 97% to nearly 200% depending on the category being investigated (National Clearinghouse on Child Abuse and Neglect Information 1996).

The United Nations estimates that 180 million people worldwide (with 4.2% of them being under fifteen years old) were taking drugs in the late 1990s (United Nations Office For Drug Control And Crime Prevention 2001). Tens of millions of those people were right here in the United States. Over 94% of the clergy surveyed by the Center on Addiction and Substance Abuse (CASA) consider substance abuse (including alcohol) an important issue among family members in their congregations (National Center On Addiction And Substance Abuse At Columbia University 1996).

Domestic violence, child abuse, and substance abuse are reaching epidemic proportions. As the world's population continues to increase and as more and more people move into metropolises and megacities, these kinds of problems will only increase. Does God care? Can the Holy Spirit make a difference in the lives of these battered, broken, and often discarded people? Does God expect his people to make a difference in the lives of people who are victims of such evil?

Abuse and addiction are not simply social problems the government needs to address. The victims of abuse and addiction are people for whom life has taken a very bad turn. Perhaps many of them were partially (or even fully) responsible for the turn their lives took. Some of them were not. Regardless of how the problems began, the end result is a human being created in God's image separated from his or her creator, hurting, alone and desperately in need of someone to step in and make a difference. I believe that God would very much like his people to be among those who step in and make a difference.

Parachurch agencies, whether orphanages, homeless shelters, or centers for victims of abuse and addiction are important avenues for outreach as we seek to participate with God in his mission in the world.

Support Services

Another category of mission work is known as support services. It should not be assumed that individuals involved in support services are not directly involved in mission work. They are. The category simply refers to aspects of mission work that may not involve direct contact with the specific people of a mission effort, but which makes the work of those who do have direct contact with them easier or more effective. I will highlight three activities categorized as support services: aviation, Christian radio or television broadcasting, and the production of Christian literature.

Aviation

Aviation as a support service of mission outreach is flying airplanes and helicopters to deliver people and supplies to areas where commercial flights may not be available or practical. One of the best known Christian aviation services is Mission Aviation Fellowship (MAF), based in Redlands, California. Begun in 1945 with a single airplane (a Waco biplane), MAF now has over seventy aircraft operating in twenty-four countries. MAF aircraft fly over 40,000 missions each year—enough miles annually to go to the moon and back nine times (Mission Aviation Fellowship 2002).

I am using MAF simply as an illustration for how important such services are. The fact that over 300 Christian and humanitarian organizations depend of MAF to transport goods and personnel to remote mission locations around the world is evidence of the need for aviation in missions. Christians who fly may find that aviation as a support service is the kind of mission work God is calling them to do.

Christian Radio and Television Broadcasting

Another important support service is Christian radio and television broadcasting. Radio and televisions can often go where missionaries cannot. Many geographic regions are politically and socially dominated by religious groups that are not friendly to Christianity. The people in those countries, however, have radios and televisions, and many of them are looking for an alternative to the religion of their culture. There are over 2 billion, 250 million people who watch television or listen to the radio with some kind of regularity each month. Over 638 million of them are tuning in to the 4,050 Christian radio and television stations broadcasting around the world (Barrett and Johnson 2002:22-23).

Christians trained in radio and television broadcasting can make an important difference in the presentation of the gospel, especially in countries or regions of the world closed to an overt Christian presence.

The Production And Distribution
Of Christian Literature

Scripture needs to be translated into local languages. Bible study material to assist people in their study of God's word must also be produced and distributed. Like aviation, and radio and television broadcasting, the production and distribution of Christian literature is a specialized field requiring training in a number of specific fields: translation, writing, local languages, printing and binding, and the various methods of transport and distribution available in different parts of the world.

The individuals involved in the production and distribution of literature may not be actively engaged with local people on a regular basis, but they are missionaries nonetheless.

Summary

I have covered a wide rage of subjects in this chapter, too many to list again in this summary. My goal was not to discuss any of them in detail, but to demonstrate the vast range of ways in which one can serve as a missionary. One does not have to be a minister or Bible teacher to be a missionary. Mechanics and bookkeepers, secretaries and English teachers, health care technicians and printers, pilots and electricians, and just about any other kind of trade or skill imaginable can be useful in missions. It is not so much a matter of what one is trained to do, but whether or not one is willing to go and serve, learning new ways of thinking and living along the way.

Going into the Field

Adequate preparation for going into the field is a crucial factor in the ultimate success or failure of missionary activity. In this chapter I will discuss some basic considerations related to preparation for going into the field.

Spiritual Preparation

Rodolfo Giron has observed that:

> Spiritual formation is essential throughout the overall development of a missionary. It does not end when the missionary arrives on the mission field either. On the contrary, a new level of spiritual development begins at this point. The real test of a missionary is whether the person is able to cope with the new spiritual realities and demands of missionary life. . . We must avoid the tendency to reduce missionary training to a mere academic exercise. To be truly effective, any training program must have at its core a very strong spiritual element (1997:31).

To be effective in participating with God in his mission, the missionary must have an intimate relationship with God. Being in a relationship with God is like being in a relationship with another human being. It involves a depth of knowing that is best described by the word intimacy. The knowing goes both ways. God knows the missionary and the missionary knows

135

God—at least, that's how it is supposed to work. The problem is that many of God's people do not really know him very well. Many people know about God; few really know him.

Intimacy with God is one goal of spiritual growth. Another is likeness. All people are created in God's image and likeness. But his image becomes dulled and distorted by sin. One of the goals of spiritual growth is getting rid of the distortion of sin so the image and likeness of God shines through in our lives. Peter talks about participation in the divine nature (2 Pet. 1:3-11). In that text he lists a number of characteristics (divine characteristics) that should be present in the lives of believers who are participating in the divine nature. A parallel passage is Galatians 5:22-23, where Paul discusses a list of characteristics that he refers to as the fruit of the Spirit. Both Peter and Paul are discussing qualities or character traits that originate with God and which, because we are created in his image, can also be character traits exhibited by human beings. The goal of spiritual formation is to allow the Holy Spirit to produce those qualities in us so we can participate in the divine nature, becoming less like our old sinful selves and more like God.

How can we become more like God? We have to want to—more than anything else in the world. Our desire to be like God must be so strong that it wins out over our desire to be self-directed and self-indulgent. Desire is the first requirement. Discipline is the second. We must take the steps that will allow the Holy Spirit to work with us, changing us into the people God wants us to be.

One of the most basic disciplines we need to develop, if the Holy Spirit is going to be able to change us, is a prayer life that is best described as *conversational meditation*. In most of our prayers we are thanking God for what he has given us and asking him for what we need or want. While this is appropriate it does not constitute the kind of communication that is characteristic of a healthy relationship. The intimacy of a relationship requires more than thanking and asking. It involves a deep-level sharing of oneself. Intimacy necessitates the tearing down of emotional walls and building bridges of trust and open communication. This is one of the things God is looking for in his relationship with people. But since we cannot sit down face to face with God, or literally hold his hand while we walk together, that kind of communication is difficult to accomplish. That is why we need to think of prayer as *conversational meditation*. We need to find time to meditate about ourselves and our relationship with God, engaging in conversation with him as we do. We need to know that even though we cannot see or touch him, God is present with us, engaging in communication with us. He listens as we speak, and will also speak to us if we will quietly and patiently listen. It will most likely not be an audible voice, but his Spirit will commune with our spirit and we will "hear" him just the same. A healthy relationship involves this kind of two-way communication.

During these times of conversational meditation we need to confess our sinfulness. Not just sinfulness in general, but our specific shortcomings when it comes to the fruits of the Spirit and the qualities of the divine nature. How do we need to change? On what do we need to focus most intently at that moment in our lives: patience, goodness, self-control, faith? What does the Spirit need to do for us? We need to analyze ourselves, identifying our strengths and weaknesses and ask the Spirit to change us.

Then comes the hard part. Once we have identified our weaknesses, admitted them, and asked the Holy Spirit to change us, we must get out of the way and let him do his work. This requires complete surrender to the will of God. Jesus stressed the necessity of self-denial, of denying our self-will, our self-determination. Our human inclination is to assert ourselves, to indulge our desire to be and do what we want. To deny one's self is to deny one of the strongest drives we have. To deny one's self is to surrender completely to God, allowing his will to override our own. What God wants is more important than what I want. Where God wants me to go is more important than where I want to go. What God wants me to do is more important than what I want to do. When we surrender completely to God, whatever God decides is all right with us.

That kind of submission results in a new depth of humility—the kind of humility Jesus demonstrated when he relinquished his grasp on his heavenly form of being God and came to earth in the form of a servant (Phil. 2:5-11). When Jesus left his heavenly culture to participate in first century Palestinian culture, Jesus became a cross-cultural missionary. He was a successful missionary because of his intimate relationship with God and because he was completely submissive and humble.

Adequate spiritual preparation is essential to a successful missions experience. Those sending missionaries into the field need to determine the spiritual readiness of those who want to go. Wanting to go and being ready to go do not always occur at the same time.

Selecting a Field

Does the missionary select the field where he or she will serve, or does God select the field where he will send the missionary? I believe that both the missionary and God are involved in the decision—or at least should be. In a healthy relationship one person does not force his or her will on the other person. God does not force us to do things we do not want to do or to go places we do not want to go. Yet if we are humbly submissive to God, we will seek his will in the matter, asking him to direct us so that we will go where we can be the most useful and effective in our service to him. He knows more than we know and can see things we can't see. We would be foolish not to ask him where he would like us to go and what he would like us to do. Since Jesus is our Master, the appropriate question is, *Master, how can I serve you?*

However, his answer may not come in a dream or vision as it did in Paul's case when he dreamed of a man from Macedonia saying, "Come over to Macedonia and help us," (Ac. 16:6-10). I am not suggesting that God does not occasionally speak directly to his servants in this manner. If God has something very specific in mind for an individual he may give that person very specific instructions. But he does not always do so. Most of the time God expects us to be involved in the process of deciding where we want to go and what kind of work we want to do—which means that we must do research.

Researching the Possibilities

There are a number of sources one can use in researching potential fields for missionary service.

Missionaries

One source is missionaries who are already serving somewhere in the world. When missionaries return from the field on furlough, they normally visit churches that support them to report on the progress of their work. In addition to speaking at local churches, missionaries also speak on college campuses and at mission workshops, lectureships and events related to missions. Listening to missionaries talk about the people with whom they work (which often includes a media presentation as well) helps mission candidates narrow their focus to a general location (Africa, India, Latin America, China) or to a specific kind of work (translation, church planting, medical missions). Talking with a missionary after his or her presentation, asking questions, expressing an interest in missions, may lead to follow-up meetings or other contacts which may further narrow one's focus.

Mission Agencies

In addition to speaking with missionaries about potential fields or kinds of work, prospective missionaries can contact mission agencies asking for information about their focus and needs. Some agencies specialize in specific kinds of work. Wycliffe, for instance, specializes in translating the Scriptures. New Tribes specializes in unreached primitive people groups. Continent of Great Cities specializes in sending mission teams into Latin American metropolises and megacities. African Inland Missions sends mission teams into Africa. Other mission agencies are less specialized, engaging in a wide variety of mission strategies.

The internet is one of the best places to begin for locating mission agencies and discovering their special interests. A simple search for "mission agencies" will yield a number of options where you can begin to research the possibilities.

Mission Journals

Another source of information on potential mission fields or specialized mission work is mission journals. There are dozens of journals, from popular to academic, from specialized to general, which can be used in gathering information about potential mission sites or specialties. *Evangelical Missions Quarterly*, the *International Bulletin of Missionary Research*, *Missiology*, and *Frontiers* are only a few of the sources available.

As with mission agencies, the internet is a good place to begin searching for journals that may be helpful in your search for ideas and information. Again, a search for "missions journals" will prove fruitful.

A Survey Trip

Research for a long term mission commitment should include a survey trip. Once you have narrowed down the possibilities and believe God is leading you to a specific location, schedule a trip to that place. Plan on spending between three and six weeks there. If possible, live how and where you would live once you arrived on the field for full time work. Experience the people and the culture to the fullest extent possible. Ask lots of questions, especially of other missionaries who may already be working there. Ask about challenges. Ask about problems. Listen, observe, ponder. Spend a lot of time with God, listening more than talking, discerning his will, his calling. A survey trip is not a vacation. It is a time to learn. It is when you lay a foundation for further reflection so you can make a long-term commitment to a particular location in your service to God.

Reaching A Decision

Before reaching a final decision about where you will serve, spend lots of time in prayer, asking for God's guidance. Of course, when you ask for God's guidance, you must listen for his answer and be willing to accept his judgment in the matter. Sometimes what you want is not what God wants. Where the Lord wants you to go is more important than where you want to go.

Pre-field Preparation

Most missionaries today go into the field as part of a mission team in connection with a mission agency that oversees a number of mission efforts. Some mission agencies are associated with a particular denomination, others are independent, interdenominational organizations recruiting and training people from various church traditions. Mission agencies have as many different approaches to missions as denominations have to Christian worship and service. While details among agencies may differ, there are also a number of similarities.

Partnering With A Mission Agency

In interviews with ten different mission agencies,[4] I found the following similarities and differences in the recruiting and training of missionaries. Most of the agencies had individuals who worked with them in recruiting potential missionary candidates. These included missionaries, former missionaries, teachers and ministers associated with the mission agency. These individuals spoke in churches and on college campuses looking for prospective missionaries. Some of the agencies also advertised in Christian publications, inviting inquiries. Prospective missionaries were asked to complete detailed applications (some up to twenty pages in length), providing details about themselves, their family, their conversion, Christian commitment, work history, health, doctrinal beliefs, and other pertinent information. Applicants can expect that as

---

[4]Agencies surveyed in January and February, 2002 included: Mission Resource Network, OMS International, African Inland Missions, NTI (New Tribes International), Pioneers, EFCM (Evangelical Free Church Missions), Christar, GEM (Greater Europe Missions), Interserve, and Send International.

many as eight references will be contacted.

Applicants were invited for interviews with the agency board or committee members and were given up to three different psychological evaluations (plus an additional evaluation for married couples), including standard personality evaluation tests and cross-cultural adaptability tests. They were also interviewed by either a psychologist or psychiatrist. Bertil Ekstrom explains the importance of psychological evaluations in the missionary selection process.

> Psychological tests can help identify emotional problems, increase candidates' self-awareness, give insight into strengths and weaknesses, and cast light on other areas that need to be dealt with. Majory Foyle, in writing about a survey she did among 121 missionaries, observed: "Fifty-four percent of the missionaries I saw complained of problems that were present long before they entered the selection process. Either they were not asked about these or overspiritualized. Only about one quarter of those who had problems prior to their selection received any help—and that was usually minimal." If candidates do not have a chance to work through their problems and wounds before leaving their secure home, there is a great risk that a deeper crisis will appear on the field (1997:191-192).

Of the agencies I interviewed, the one not using psychological evaluations required anywhere from two to four years training with their staff before sending missionaries to the field, so they felt they knew their missionaries (their strengths, weaknesses and psychological makeup) quite well without the benefit of evaluations.

Agencies may vary considerably in their selection and

evaluation process. Kath Donovan and Ruth Myors suggest twelve important considerations in the selection process: past history, stress management, relationships, self-expression, family of origin, motivation, time management, marriage relationship, children, sensitive issues, psychological testing, and references (1997:68-70). Most agencies will take most of those factors into consideration in their selection process.

Once a candidate is accepted, pre-field training begins. Though details of training differ from agency to agency, the general focus is on Bible knowledge, cross-cultural awareness, language learning skills, fundraising techniques, spiritual growth, conflict management, and mission strategies. Training may last anywhere from a few weeks, to two to four years, depending on the agency. Two to six weeks of intense pre-field training appear to be the average, with some agencies using outside mission training agencies (institutes or schools) rather than attempting to train candidates themselves.

In addition to pre-field training, additional training on the field by people already there (assuming a work is not a brand new pioneering work where there are no other people on the field) brings the total training for a number of agencies to around six months. New Tribes International has the longest pre-field training requirements (two to four years, depending on previous Bible training). Since New Tribes works exclusively with primitive (usually isolated) tribes that are still unreached for Christ, they feel their missionaries need additional training. Agencies that require less pre-field training than New Tribes require language learning and on-going field training in cultural issues after arrival on the field.

Some agencies, depending on a candidate's previous training, may suggest that he or she enroll in an undergraduate or graduate missions training program as pre-field training. Even missionaries who already have an undergraduate or graduate degree in missions, can expect to receive some additional training before arriving on the field.

A valuable test which individual agencies may or may not

use in their pre-field training is the Basic Values Questionnaire (Lingenfelter and Mayers 1986:27-36). It is designed to help missionaries understand their own basic value system (which is part of their worldview). The value of this test (and others like it) is in assisting missionaries in becoming aware of the deeply rooted assumptions by which they regulate their lives. Understanding how and why they act as they do in their own culture helps missionaries understand how and why people in other cultures act as they do and enables missionaries to adapt to the value system of their new culture more easily. If tests like the Basic Values Questionnaire are not used by a mission agency in their pre-field training, I suggest that missionaries purchase Lingenfelter's and Mayers' book, *Ministering Cross-Culturally*, and take the test themselves.

As for cultural information on the site where one is going, a website called Culture Grams (www.culturegrams.com) provides a basic cultural overview of most countries. A four volume set of books which is also helpful is *Countries And Their Cultures* (Melvin Ember and Carol Ember 2000). Sources like these will provide a basic overview of a country's culture. Most culture learning, however, will occur on the field. The goal of pre-field cultural awareness training is to help missionaries begin thinking about the different cultural perspectives they will encounter and begin developing a flexibility in their thinking. Missionaries must develop the ability to appreciate the beauty and value of the new culture in which they will live and work and not constantly compare it to their own culture.

A Word Of Caution And Encouragement

At this point I would like to add a word of encouragement about anthropological training in cross-cultural awareness. Mission agencies that appreciate the importance of cross-

145

cultural awareness and include some exposure to it in their pre-field orientation programs are to be congratulated. However, a few days of cross-cultural awareness training as part of a two or three week orientation is simply not enough.

Cross-cultural training includes an awareness of basic social concerns in a given culture. For instance, in many cultures it is highly inappropriate to pass something to someone else with your left hand. It is also inappropriate to get down to business right away when meeting with someone (as most Americans like to do) instead of chatting informally for a while (sometimes forty-five minutes to an hour) before getting around to the agenda. Learning how to behave appropriately in one's new culture is an important part of cross-cultural awareness. But it is not the most important part. The most important issue of cross-cultural awareness is learning the worldview of the people among whom one will be working, and becoming aware of one's own worldview assumptions and understanding that while those assumptions may be the foundation of your cultural patterns, they are not the foundations of everyone else's cultural patterns.

This is especially true when it comes to the way we interpret and apply the Scriptures. Our tendency is to think that the theological conclusions we have arrived at in the West represent the only way to understand and apply the Scriptures. Nothing could be further from the truth. Most mission agencies have expectations regarding Bible training for their missionaries, many of them requiring at least thirty hours of college level Bible study. That is commendable. But the Bible training most missionaries receive is traditional Bible training from a Western theological perspective, not from a cross-cultural perspective. In Chapter 3, I discussed the importance of contextualization and ethnotheologizing. My point there and here is that missionaries must be able to lay aside (as much as is humanly possible) their own culturally impacted theological perspective and develop the ability to interpret and apply the Scriptures from the worldview perspective of the people among whom they are working. To do this takes both training and time, much more time than can be allotted in a few days of cross-cultural awareness training in a two or three week orientation.

I would encourage missionaries to set aside the necessary time and funds to take classes in anthropology and contextualization designed to help them work through the delicate issues related to cross-cultural hermeneutics (also known as ethnohermeneutics). And I would encourage mission agencies to require training in anthropology and contextualization so that missionaries do not continue to teach a Western interpretation of Scripture in non-Western cultures.

If there is simply not enough time and money to take courses in anthropology and contextualization, missionaries should at least purchase and read books which address these issues. A partial list of these is available in Appendix A.

Raising Support

Raising support is not an easy job. Some missionaries compare it to begging. Thinking of it in those terms only makes the job harder and increases the likelihood that the wrong message will be communicated in the fundraising process. Betty Barnett has written a fine book on fundraising that every missionary should read. She calls it, *Friend Raising: Building A Missionary Support Team That Lasts* (1991). A similar book on fundraising is by William Dillon, *People Raising: A Practical Guide To Raising Support* (1993).

One of the points Barnett makes in her book is that missionaries must realize that they are working together with God and his people to accomplish God's purpose in the world. We cannot live independent of God and we should not want to live independent of his people. Giving others an opportunity to participate with us in a particular mission is not begging. It is giving them an opportunity to participate, to serve. Asking for money and giving someone an opportunity to participate is not the same thing. The missionary's perception of the fundraising process makes an enormous difference in his or her success.

Another point Barnett makes is that the focus should be on relationships not on money. That is why she refers to *friend*raising rather than *fund*raising. If we are concerned about the people we speak to about missions rather than their money, that concern will be evident and will allow the missionary to build a relationship with a person instead of banking another donation. Developing relationships with people who are interested in your work, who will pray for you and the people to whom you minister is the most important contribution people can make to your work. Those who become friends and co-laborers in your work will also help support you financially. Your goal should be to make mission partners (friends), not to raise money. When you create mission partners, the money will follow.

How does one go about creating mission partners? Barnett discusses four pillars in building a missionary support team: friend raising, generosity, communication and prayer with promises (1991:19). I agree with her completely, but would break the process down into two basic steps: 1) telling your story and, 2) building and maintaining relationships.

To get people interested in the work you want to do you must tell your story. Where do you want to go? What do you want to do? Why do you want to do it? Your reasons may seem obvious to you, but they may not be to others. In the process of telling your story, tell stories about others. Who are the people among whom you will be working? What are they like? Why do they need you to do what you are proposing to do? Show lots of pictures. The people you want to interest in your mission project need to hear and see what you are talking about.

Who do you tell your story to? Start with your family and friends. Then go to the leaders in your church. Ask to be able to speak to the church about your plans. From your local church, look for opportunities in other churches. Make phone calls and write letters to church leaders, asking for an opportunity to talk about a mission opportunity.

Outline your presentation, making sure you anticipate and answer all the important questions. Practice what you are going to say. Know what stories you are going to tell, what pictures you are going to show and where in your presentation you will show them. Create a Power Point presentation and practice your presentation.

As you tell your stories, make it clear that you are inviting the people listening to participate with you in your ministry. The most important way they can participate with you is to pray about the work, asking for God's blessing on you and the people with whom you will be working. God's blessing is more important than all the money you could ever raise. You want your mission partners to pray with you and for you about your work. Also ask them to pray for God's guidance about their financial participation in the work. You are not asking them to contribute to your work, you are asking them to ask God about his will regarding their financial participation in your work. Your will and their will is not the issue. God's will is what matters most.

Tell your story and ask for prayers. Ask for prayers for you and the mission you want to be involved in, and ask them to pray regarding their financial participation in the project. But make it clear that the most important thing is their friendship, their interest in your work and their willingness to pray for you. That is Part 1, telling your story. Part 2 is building and maintaining relationships.

As you travel from place to place telling your story, you encounter people who will want to talk with you. Take the time to listen to them. Spend time getting to know them. Getting a check from them is not your goal. Being a friend is. Write down their name and address. Get their phone number. Later in the week write them a personal note, thanking them for their interest in your work. Tell them about specific things you would like for them to pray about. Ask them how you can pray for them. Friendship is a two-way process. If they are going to pray for you, you must also pray for them. If they are going to be your friend, you must also be theirs.

As you repeat the process over and over again, your list of friends will grow. So will your income. Not all of your mission friends will send you money, but many of them will. Some will send regular support, others will send special gifts as God blesses them. Regardless of how much money they send or how often, if you consider them your friends you will want to communicate with them. A newsletter every couple of months is a good way to keep in touch. Make it personal. Include pictures. Tell stories. Perhaps you can even take the time to include a personal hand written note on each one. A handwritten note to a specific person says so much more than an impersonal newsletter. It takes time, but that is the nature of a relationship.

Friendraising is better than fundraising. It is better for you and better for the people who will participate with you in your ministry. When you take time to build ministry friends, God will bless your efforts and you will have the money you need when you need it.

The Independent Missionary

Some Christian traditions have always been fiercely independent. Members of those loosely connected churches may not be comfortable being associated with an agency. They may prefer to deal with an eldership in a local congregation. These missionaries pray for God's guidance in selecting a field and then set about finding an eldership who will serve as their sponsoring church, providing as much of the missionary's total support as their congregational budget will allow. If their sponsoring church cannot support them fully, the missionary will raise the balance of his or her support from other churches and individuals and then set out for the field. They may be part of a larger team, or may be working on their own. The advisability of working without a team and a support agency (beyond the local church back home) may be questionable, but it is a fact of life for many missionaries. For independent missionaries it is even more important to have a strong network of friends (mission partners) praying for them and their work.

It is also important that the supporting church be very involved in the mission project. Putting money into the work is not enough. Leaders in the supporting church have to be interested in the work, seeing it as an extension of their local work. Independent missionaries need to encourage as much involvement as possible. One or more of the leaders of the supporting church needs to visit the field, learning about the nature of the work, the needs of the people and the needs of the missionary. There is nothing wrong with being "independent" if that is part of the theological tradition one is from. However, ministry cannot be carried out in isolation, and independence does not mean independence from God or his people. It does not mean working without the support and input of others. Being part of the body of Christ means being connected to others who also participate with God in accomplishing his mission in the world.

Stewardship

A discussion about pre-field preparation is a good place to talk briefly about stewardship. Stewardship is an important part of the Christian life. It is especially important for missionaries who raise support from others in order to engage in full-time ministry.

Stewardship may be defined differently depending on one's family background. For many, stewardship means being responsible with one's resources. For some, however, stewardship seems to imply frugality. I want to suggest that stewardship does not necessarily imply frugality. The Greek word translated as steward is *oikonomos*, which means basically a manager, superintendent, or overseer. Being a good steward or manager of one's financial resources does not mean always buying the least expensive. This is an important and sometimes difficult lesson for missionaries to learn.

By its very nature, mission work requires travel. Travel is hard on both body and belongings. Inexpensive items may be adequate in less stressful circumstances, but buying less expensive items to be used on the mission field can often turn out to be more expensive in the long run because they have to be replaced, or they do not perform adequately. Take electronic equipment as an example. Some missionaries where I served in Nigeria had purchased less expensive laptop computers loaded with off-brand software. They did this to save money. However, the equipment did not always work as well as the better built name brand machines and the software was not as compatible as they had been led to believe. The few hundred dollars they had saved (which averaged out to pennies a day over several years on the field) did not, at that point, appear to have been very good stewardship.

Stewardship should not be equated with less expensive or cheap. It should be equated with the best use of one's available resources. For the missionary, that often means having very good quality, current technology electronic equipment: a cell phone capable of international calls, a laptop computer, perhaps a printer and a scanner, and a high quality digital camera. Your mission work may be people centered rather than task oriented. That is certainly appropriate. But missionaries still have tasks to perform. They have to communicate with the folks back home as well as with other missionaries, mission agencies and perhaps, depending on their situation, a college or seminary. One should not buy off-brand or less expensive equipment in the name of good stewardship only to regret it later when the equipment does not perform adequately.

The Challenges of Life as a Missionary

All the training and preparation, the raising of spiritual and financial support, and the hours of prayer come together in the trip to the airport. Many months, and possibly several years of plans, hopes and dreams are becoming a reality. By the time missionaries board the plane they have already made many sacrifices and have overcome many obstacles. They are ready for the Lord to use them in his service. Little can compare to the excitement of bidding family and friends farewell as missionaries leave for the mission field to which the Lord has called them. It may be the most exciting day of their lives. There will be many exciting days as they encounter the new culture in which they will be living. There will be many challenges. They will be prepared for some of them, but not for all of them. In this section, I want to highlight some of the challenges missionaries will face in the process of living life as a missionary.

Settling In

The first few weeks (or months) of life in a new culture is exciting. The new missionary's days will be filled with the wonders of their new home. There will be new sights, new sounds, new smells. The food will be different. The climate will be different. People will dress differently, talk differently and act differently. They will think very differently about things as well, though the new missionary may not be fully aware of this for a while. Their house will be different. Their daily routine will be different. The way they get around and the places they go will be different. At first the differences will be exotic, exciting, fun. The missionaries will be curious, asking questions, noticing all the little differences in how people live in this new place. They will learn the local greetings, sample the local food. They will learn about the local currency and observe marketplace interaction so they can fit in as they begin to settle in. At first, it will almost be like a vacation. It will be wonderful. This is the early stages of the *acculturation* process.

"Acculturation is the process of culture change set in motion by the meeting of two autonomous cultural systems" (Glick 1997:1). In the simplest terms, acculturation is the process of learning a second culture.

Van Rheenen suggests that there are three stages to the acculturation process: the glamour stage (also known as the honeymoon stage), the rejection stage, and the identification stage (1996:87). Arriving on the field and settling in are part of the glamour stage when everything is new, interesting and exciting. But the excitement will eventually give way to frustration and dissatisfaction as you enter the second stage of the acculturation process: rejection. The symptoms of this stage of the process are often referred to as culture shock.

Culture Shock

Kraft describes culture shock, or culture stress, as:

> the condition experienced by nearly everyone at the start of life in a different culture, in which one feels off balance, unable to predict what people's reactions will be when one does or says something. It is a real psychological response to very real perceptions and must be taken seriously (2000:256).

Hiebert describes culture shock as "the disorientation we experience when all the cultural maps and guidelines we learned as children no longer work," (1985:66).

As the newness and excitement of our new home wears off and we attempt to settle into a daily routine, we begin to feel an uneasiness. The old familiar cultural landscape which we understood and with which we identified is gone. Nothing is the same. The simple things we used to do without giving them much thought, such as going to the store, going to the post office, having a conversation with your neighbor, listening to the radio, watching television, or going to a restaurant, become major challenges that take a great deal of time and energy, often leaving the new missionary frustrated and uneasy.

One afternoon while living in Nigeria, my seventeen year old son and I went into to local market to buy paint thinner. We went to a merchant who sold tools, paintbrushes and other items. It was the Nigerian equivalent to a hardware store. The merchant spoke English, as did all the merchants in the marketplace. We asked for paint thinner. His confused expression told us we were not starting off well. Slowly he shook his head and pointed, sending us to another shop in the marketplace which would have what we wanted. We went to the second merchant and asked for paint thinner. The merchant's furrowed brow and confused expression told us that we were probably not going to get what we wanted from him, either. He told us we needed to go to the stationary shop. Stationary? He pointed, nodded emphatically, and said, "stationary."

We went to the stationary merchant and asked for paint thinner, explaining that another merchant told us he had paint thinner. The merchant was all smiles. "Yes," he said, nodding happily. We did not understand why you would buy paint thinner from the stationary merchant, but if that's the way it worked in Nigeria, that was all right with us. We didn't care where we got it, we just needed some paint thinner. The happy merchant turned and went to get our paint thinner. Returning with a box of pencils, he handed it to us with a smile and a sense of accomplishment. My son and I were both confused. We had asked for paint thinner and he had brought us a box of pencils. I shook my head, handing the box of pencils back to him, saying, "paint thinner." He frowned as he shook his head, his disappointment obvious.

I suggested to my son that we try another section of the marketplace. I remembered another "hardware store" where the merchant sold paint. Surely he would have paint thinner. We made our way across the crowded market to the other merchant and asked for paint thinner. He, too, frowned in consternation, unsure of what we were asking for. "Paint thinner," I said impatiently as my frustration mounted. There were cans of paint sitting on the shelf behind him. This should have been a simple task. If they sold paint they had to have paint thinner.

Making signs with my hands, pouring imaginary paint thinner into an imaginary can of paint and stirring it up, I repeated the words he should have understood, "Paint thinner... Thinner." That did it. When I said "thinner" his face suddenly lit up. "Oh, thinner," he said emphatically, calling it by it's proper name. "Thinner." "Yes," he said, nodding as he turned and picked up a can of paint thinner. The can he handed me said *Paint Thinner* right on the front of it. But the Nigerians did not call it *paint* thinner. They called it simply *thinner*. When I said *paint thinner* they had no idea what I wanted. A simple task that should have taken less than five minutes took over an hour.

It was a frustrating experience that resulted in culture stress. When experiences such as the paint thinner incident (as it is referred to in our family) happen day after day (sometimes several times a day!), the new missionary's level of frustration can become and remain dangerously high. If the problem of culture stress is not dealt with effectively, the missionary may become dysfunctional, withdrawing from contact with the local people, unable to do the very thing he or she went there to do.

What can be done about culture stress? There are several things to be done, each involving a prayerful, submissive attitude. First, missionaries must ask God to help them develop a greater sense of self-awareness. Some people require a great deal of structure and familiarity in their lives. When they find themselves in a situation where the familiar structures are missing, they become frustrated, angry or frightened. Other people seem to be able to cope with less structure and familiarity more effectively. Missionaries need to know if they are the kind of people who require more or less structure and familiarity. The psychological evaluations that are often part of one's pre-field training are also helpful in this regard. Missionaries who realize that they are more likely to become frustrated in situations where the familiar things of life are missing are better prepared to cope with the inevitable.

Second, missionaries need to pray for patience and the courage not to become upset when coping with the unfamiliar. They need to pray that God will help them be pliable rather than rigid people. Being willing to learn means being willing to change.

Third, missionaries need to pray that they will be good culture learners. Missionaries, like all people, spend the first years of their lives learning the culture of their home and their people. Then, at twenty, thirty, forty or fifty years old they find themselves having to learn another culture (often including a new language). They must become little children again, learning to speak, learning to interact with their new environment and with people, learning what is expected of them and what to expect of others. Some people enjoy learning. It is fun and easy for them. Others do not enjoy learning, especially if it seems to require unlearning one behavior or expectation and replacing it with another—which is what learning a new culture is about. Missionaries need to pray that God will help them be good culture learners.

Fourth, missionaries must pray for the courage to interact with their new cultural surroundings, learning something new everyday. Missionaries must overcome the tendency to hold on to the old, closing themselves off from the new. They must go out and embrace the new, learning the language and the customs, getting to know the people. They must be willing to be laughed at as they make mistakes. They must learn to trust God, to trust themselves and their new neighbors.

The most important tool for learning the new culture is learning the language. The key to learning how people think, and thus understanding their worldview, is learning their language. When missionaries learn to speak as the local people speak, they will learn to think as the local people think. They will begin to see the world through the eyes of the local people. As the new culture begins to make sense, the missionary will become comfortable, as one is comfortable in his or her own culture.

Language Learning

Having mentioned language learning as part of the culture learning process, and as a way to cope with and overcome culture stress, I also want to discuss it as an essential part of the missionary's early in-field training.

Learning the language of the people is essential. Why? There are several reasons. First, you can't really understand a people's worldview and culture if you don't understand their language, for their language is an expression of their worldview and culture. Or to say it another way, a people's language is the most accurate way their unique worldview and culture is expressed or communicated.

Second, you cannot communicate effectively with a person if you do not speak his or her language. What about using a translator? Communication by means of a translator may be better than no communication at all, but it is far from being effective person-to-person communication. The cross-cultural communication process requires communicators to encode messages with the receptor's worldview in mind, knowing that receptors must infer the communicator's intended meaning. The process is difficult enough as it is without inserting a translator into the equation. The translator must decode the communicator's message, infer his or her meaning (that is, decide what he thinks the communicator is saying), and then re-encode the message into the receptor's language in a way that will allow the receptor to infer a meaning similar to that of the communicator—or more precisely, with what the translator thought the communicator meant. All communication is complicated and imprecise. Communicating through a translator is even more complicated and imprecise. If you want to communicate effectively with an individual you need to learn to speak that person's language.

Third, language learning is essential because God has

demonstrated for us that speaking to a person in his or her own language is the appropriate way to communicate with that person. When God spoke to Adam and Eve he did not use a translator. When he spoke to Noah, Moses and Abraham he did not use a translator. When God decided to come to the Jewish people in the person of Jesus, he spoke Aramaic, the language common to the Jews of that day. In the person of Jesus, God became one of the people, learning their culture, speaking their language, living as one of them. Jesus was not a foreigner. Jesus was one of the people. He spoke their language. When the church was established and the Holy Spirit distributed special gifts to the believers, one of the gifts he gave individuals was the ability to speak in a language (or languages) those individuals had never learned. Why? So believers could speak to others about God in their own language.

Learning the language is the most basic way missionaries become one of the people. It may not be possible for missionaries to live in the kind of house local people live in. It may not be possible for missionaries to adopt completely the dietary habits of local people. Missionaries may not be completely comfortable dressing as the local people dress. But one thing missionaries can do which will allow them to identify with the people at the most basic level of human-to-human relationship is to learn their language. It takes time. It is difficult and frustrating. But it is worth it.

What are the keys to effective language learning? There may be others, but two of the most important are desire and learning how to learn. Desire is important because if we really want to do a thing we will find a way to do it. Take the victims of spinal cord accidents as examples. Many individuals who have suffered severe spinal cord injuries, who have faced living the rest of their lives in a wheelchair, have, with a great deal of determination (and the help of God), overcome their disability and learned to walk again. They made a decision that they would walk again. And whatever else may have been involved in their ultimate victory over their disability, part of their equation for success was their determination. People throughout the world overcome tremendous odds and realize their dreams each day because of desire and determination. People accomplish amazing things simply because they want to. If missionaries are determined to learn the local language of the people, and if they ask God to help them, what is to stop them?

A second key ingredient in language acquisition is learning how to learn. Elizabeth S. Brewster is a specialist in second language acquisition. In her book, *Language Acquisition Made Practical* (co-authored with her late husband, Tom), Dr. Brewster lays out an easy to follow, step-by-step procedure for learning a language. Her "Learning Cycle" involves a four step process including "getting, practicing, using and evaluating" (1976:1). Brewster points out that;

> a large percentage of the world's population speaks more than one language—probably well over half. Multitudes of illiterates are multilingual without the benefit of a language school. They learned the language because they *used* the language. The main place for learning a language is in the streets and homes of the community, (1976:5).

You already know how to learn a language because you have already learned one. The trick is to remember how you learned your native language as a child, and, utilizing those same basic skills, learn another language. Brewster's book helps you do that.

Learning the language of the people to whom you want to tell the story of Jesus is one of the most crucial aspects of your training and preparation. It takes time. It is not easy. It can be frustrating and even humiliating, for in the early stages you make many mistakes. Even the local children can speak more correctly than you. Most missionaries would rather get right to work doing what they went to the mission field to do. But until you can speak to the people in their language, you cannot do effectively what you became a missionary to do. You simply must take the time to learn the language.

Living and Working with Missionaries

Missionaries are wonderful people. They are dedicated, committed, sacrificial people. They have left their homes and families to serve their Lord, often in cultures very different from their own. Missionaries deserve all the honor and recognition we can give them. But having said that, it is also important to remember that missionaries are just people—plain old ordinary sinful people, like everyone else on planet earth. They are forgiven people, but they are far from being perfect people. They are just as far from perfect as are you and I. And what happens when you put a group of imperfect people together in close proximity to one another, especially in an environment that includes the stresses of cross-cultural interaction? Sometimes (not often, but sometimes) the hardest part of being a missionary is getting along with other missionaries with whom you work.

Many mission agencies, recognizing the need for conflict management skills, include training in conflict resolution in their pre-field training. Those agencies that do not will likely suffer a higher rate of attrition among their missionaries than those that do. Research suggests that nearly 17% of problems that lead to missionary attrition are related to some form of conflict between missionaries. Conversely, when missionaries are asked what factors contribute to long and satisfying field service, 54% say good relationships are part of the mix (Brierley 1997:85-103).

Another interesting feature of research related to conflict management has to do with the way missionaries of different ages deal with conflict. Missionaries over 50 tend to either deny that there is a problem or attempt to deal with it in an indirect way. Younger missionaries, between 30 and 50 years old, tend to want to clarify issues and work towards a resolution. Missionaries under 30 tend to be more direct, addressing issues openly without reservation in order to resolve difficulties (Donovan and Myors 1997: 41-73). A mission team with members who represent different generations must be aware of generational differences toward the management of conflict. Different approaches to managing conflict can lead to additional conflict!

Conflict management (or the lack of awareness and skill in that area) can make mission work a painful and disappointing experience. However, having said that, I also want to say that I do not believe that missionaries have any more of a problem with conflict management than any other group of people working in close proximity to one another. The cross-cultural setting in which the conflict occurs may be a complicating factor, but with proper training and spiritual maturity the issues can often be resolved to everyone's satisfaction. The presence of conflict does not automatically mean that the mission will fail.

Another factor in the mix of field experiences that impacts how a group of missionaries get along is related to physical difficulties they have to endure. When my family and I were in Nigeria, there were a total of five couples and two single men who lived and worked in close proximity on the campus of a Christian college. All three of the age ranges mentioned above were represented. We had different ideas about what needed to be done and how. For instance, we had different views on the appropriateness of "giving gifts" to government officials in order to grease the wheels of bureaucracy. Some of us (including me) saw the practice as nothing less than bribery. Other concluded that it was simply the way business was done and that it was no different than leaving a tip for a waiter or waitress in a restaurant. We had different (and strong opinions) about teaching methodologies and the direction the college should take in seeking government accreditation. Administrative meetings were often tense and uncomfortable due to the differences between Americans and Nigerians regarding proper administrative methodology.

At one point during our time in Nigeria, fear among the general population (for a number of political reasons) that the value of the local currency (the naira) was about to drop caused everyone to stop trading naira for dollars. All the missionaries had plenty of American money. But we could not spend it in Nigeria. Normally we would write a check each month to a local money-changer to acquire the naira we need to buy food and other necessities. When we could not trade our dollars for naira we could not buy food. After a couple of weeks, things began to get uncomfortable. We had to pool our resources to have sufficient food. One family had purchased a large quantity of beans. Another a large quantity of sugar. Our family had quite a bit of flour. Someone else had extra reserves of rice. Suddenly some of our differences of opinion regarding academic matters did not seem so important. We shared our flour and sugar, rice and beans, and over the next week or so everyone had enough to eat. The experience brought us closer together and eased tensions for a while. The problems did not go away. But people who share food to keep from going hungry learn to be more tolerant of one another.

Conflict between missionaries can be a real problem on the mission field. Skills in conflict resolution are essential. So is patience and tolerance. Sometimes the circumstances in which missionaries find themselves force them to be more patient and tolerant of each other.

Communicating with Supporters:
A Picture is Worth a Thousand Words

In a previous section I talked about raising support. This is often referred to as fundraising. Barnett prefers the term *friendraising*. I believe she is right in her focus on relationships as the foundation for individuals or churches becoming partners with the missionary in the Lord's work. Individuals and churches support missionaries because they have formed a relationship with that missionary. Communication is an essential and foundational aspect of any relationship, including the missionary/supporter relationship.

In another previous section, I discussed the importance of buying good electronic equipment to take into the field. This is especially important if your work is in more remote areas where equipment may not be available. My reason for encouraging additional expense in this regard has to do not only with dependability, but with the ability to communicate effectively. Along with a cell phone capable of international calls and a current computer and peripherals, a good quality digital camera is essential. Why? Because you need to include photos in your monthly newsletters. Seeing pictures of you, the setting in which you work, and the local people among whom you work keeps you and the importance of your mission in the minds and hearts of your friends and supporters.

A regular newsletter is essential if you want your supporters to think about you, pray for you, and maintain regular support. Barnett prefers writing personal letters to supporters. I do not feel personal letters are necessary (though they are certainly appropriate if a missionary is inclined to write them), but a regular newsletter (perhaps monthly) is essential. You need to tell interesting stories about what is going on in your work. Tell stories about people and circumstances. Tell stories about struggles and victories. Ask for prayers for yourself and for the individuals with whom you are working. Include several photos of yourself and others in each newsletter. This is why a digital camera is important, so you can download high quality photos directly into your newsletter and print them on a good quality printer.

It may be difficult for you to send your newsletters out directly from where you are. You may find it is simpler to send an original copy to someone in the States so they can duplicate it and send it out to everyone on your list of supporters. You may be able to e-mail your newsletter to some of your supporters. However, there are still many older Christians who are not comfortable with computers. Electronic communication is great, but many people still need to get a printed copy in the mail.

Summary

I began this chapter by discussing the importance of spiritual preparation of the missionary. You can't lead other people into a deep, satisfying relationship with God if you don't have one yourself. Knowing about God is not the same as knowing God. The most important preparation for any missionary, even more important than cross-cultural awareness and college level Bible training, is a deep and abiding relationship with God.

Field selection is a major step in the mission process. Where you serve has a great deal to do with how you serve. Some fields may be a more compatible fit with your particular gifts and talents than others. God and the missionary work together in selecting a field of service. The missionary should always seek God's guidance in the choice of a place to serve, but should not expect the Lord to do all the work. Research is an important part of the selection process. Other missionaries, mission agencies, and mission journals can be helpful in gathering information that will help missionaries select a number of options for prayerful consideration. Before a decision is made regarding a location, a survey trip is essential.

Pre-field preparation is crucial for a successful mission tour. Training in cross-cultural awareness, Bible, conflict management, language learning, strategy and a number of other important issues can make the different between success or failure, satisfaction or dissatisfaction.

There are many decisions to be made before one leaves for the field. There are a number of logistical problems to be addressed, and potential difficulties to be aware of. Support must be raised. Equipment and other supplies must be purchased. Prayers must be prayed and answers must come—all before the missionary steps foot on the field. The importance of thorough pre-field preparation cannot be stressed too much.

I have also discussed the challenges of living life as a missionary. My goal is not to discourage anyone, but to be realistic and prepare readers for the kinds of difficulties one encounters when one lives and works closely with people in a cross-cultural setting. The challenges of adjusting to a new culture and learning a new language are complicated when missionaries get upset with one another. Missionaries are wonderful, sacrificial, committed people. Like all believers, they are spiritual works-in-process, as the Holy Spirit helps them become more like God. Some of them are closer to that goal than others. When you put less-than-perfect people together in close proximity to one another problems will develop. Conflict resolution skills become essential.

The last section in this chapter has to do with communicating with supporters. Communicating with supporters is what makes ongoing mission service possible. Missionaries need to schedule specific time for preparing newsletters which include personal stories about themselves and the people with whom they are working. Newsletters also need to include photos because the saying is true: a picture is worth a thousand words.

In the next chapter, I will discuss ways in which missionaries can participate and contribute to the global missionary community.

Chapter 7

Being Part of the Larger Missionary/Missiological Community

Missionaries, whether working alone or as part of a mission team, are members of the Lord's one universal church, participating with God in carrying out his purpose in the world. As part of the larger missionary or missiological community that spans the globe, missionaries (even new ones) can make a contribution to that community and can benefit from what that community has to offer. This chapter is about ways missionaries can contribute to and benefit from the global missions community.

Unity and Cooperation

Missionaries are not in competition with one another for the souls of lost people. It is important that Christians remember: 1) that Jesus wanted his followers to be united, 2) that Paul condemned the division that existed in first century churches, 3) that he suggested a framework or formula which could serve as the basis for unity among believers, and 4) that mature, Spirit-led believers will strive to foster a spirit of unity and cooperation amongst themselves.

Jesus' Prayer for Unity

"I am praying not only for these disciples but

also for all who will ever believe in me because of their testimony. My prayer for all of them is that they will be one, just as you and I are one, Father—that just as you are in me and I am in you, so they will be in us, and the world will believe you sent me" (Jn. 17:20-21 NLT)

Jesus prayed for oneness among his followers. Historically the church has not achieved the unity Jesus hoped for. Division in one form or another has marred the body of Christ almost from the beginning. The church today, as in every generation, is faced with a simple question: Shall we honor Jesus' prayer for unity? God does not force people do what he wants them to do. We are free to choose to obey or disobey, to cooperate with God or rebel against his will. Normally we think of God as the one who answers prayer. Generally speaking, that is true. Yet in the case of Jesus' prayer for unity, whether or not his prayer is answered depends a great deal on us—on our willingness to lay aside our own stubborn will, reflected in the divisions that now characterize the universal church, and submit to God, emphasizing and working toward unity in the body.

Jesus' prayer for unity has special significance for missions since Jesus said that oneness among his followers would impact the world's assessment of his identity and mission. The division that exists in the Christian church has been cited by unbelievers as a factor in their unwillingness to respond favorably to the good news. Even if Christians object, saying that such a comment is merely an excuse for unbelief, the reality of a divided church is ever present. Shall we continue to give unbelievers another reason for their unbelief? Or shall we trust that Jesus knew what he was talking about when he said that unity among his followers would result in belief? If for no other reason, missionaries ought to work toward unity simply because Jesus wanted his followers to be one.

Paul's Condemnation of Division

> *Now, dear brothers and sisters, I appeal to you by the authority of the Lord Jesus Christ to stop arguing among yourselves. Let there be real harmony so there won't be divisions in the church. I plead with you to be of one mind, united in thought and purpose. For some members of Chloe's household have told me about your arguments, dear brothers and sisters. Some of you are saying, "I am a follower of Paul." Others are saying, "I follow Apollos," or "I follow Peter," or "I follow only Christ." Can Christ be divided into pieces? Was I, Paul, crucified for you? Were any of you baptized in the name of Paul?* (1 Cor. 1:10-14 NLT)

The division that existed in the church at Corinth has, unfortunately, been characteristic of the body of Christ throughout the ages. When Jesus said, "*I will build my church,*" a divided body was not what he had in mind. In 1 Corinthians 12:12-20, Paul used the metaphor of the body to describe the church. He said there was one body that had many different parts. Though he was speaking about individuals in a local church, his illustration makes it clear that unity does not require uniformity. A body has many different parts that function separately, each doing the job it was designed to do. But each part works in conjunction with every other part, cooperating together so the body can function as one unit. There is no uniformity, but there is unity. There is cooperation and coordination. We joke about being able to walk and chew gum at the same time. But we could not do that if there was no cooperation and coordination (unity) between the various parts of our body.

That is why Paul condemned the division that split the church in Corinth. That division kept the church there from functioning as a coordinated unit. Their lack of unity kept them from working together in partnership with God to the fullest extent, enabling them to achieve his purpose in that ancient city. Jesus said, *"Your love for one another will prove to the world that you are my disciples"* (Jn. 14:35 NLT). The division that existed in the church in Corinth did not grow of the love they should have had for one another. Division is always counter-productive.

A Scriptural Formula for Unity

When Paul wrote to the believers in the region of Ephesus, one of the needs he addressed was the need for unity. He said:

> *Therefore I, a prisoner for serving the Lord, beg you to lead a life worthy of your calling, for you have been called by God. Be humble and gentle. Be patient with each other, making allowance for each other's faults because of your love. Always keep yourselves united in the Holy Spirit, and bind yourselves together with peace.*
>
> *We are all one body, we have the same Spirit, and we have all been called to the same glorious future. There is only one Lord, one faith, one baptism, and there is only one God and Father, who is over us all and in us all and living through us all* (Eph. 4:1-6 NLT).

Notice the ingredients in Paul's formula for unity. Believers are to be humble and gentle, patient and tolerant, bound together in the peaceful unity of the Holy Spirit. Why? Because the nature of the faith we have and of the things in which we participate is oneness. There is only one body, one Spirit, one calling, one Lord, one faith, one baptism and one God. The nature of Christianity is oneness. Christians, therefore, ought to be one. Notice also that Paul speaks of being united in the Holy Spirit. The Spirit's goal is the oneness for which Jesus prayed. The Holy Spirit does not cause division in the body of Christ. Following the Spirit does not lead to division. Not following the Spirit leads to division. Shall believers today continue to perpetuate the division caused by believers of previous generations? Or shall we follow the Holy Spirit as he leads us into peace and unity? Scripture provides us with a formula for unity. Whether or not we apply the formula is up to us.

A Cooperative Spirit

Mission work can be a lonely endeavor. While many churches or mission agencies will deploy teams of missionaries to work together, there are still lots of missionaries throughout the world working by themselves. When a missionary is a long way from home, family, and friends, surrounded by people of a different culture, few of whom may yet share the missionary's faith, the fellowship of mature believers from home can provide a point of contact that refreshes the soul and nourishes the spirit. One of the most important reasons for missionaries to work toward unity is so they can enjoy the fellowship of other believers, even if they are not of the same religious tradition.

Beyond the obvious benefits of fellowship in the mission field, another benefit of unity is the possibility of coordinated efforts and shared resources. If we serve the same Lord and we have the same goal, can we not work together to accomplish the task God has given us? We may have different opinions on some matters, and we may approach some things from a different perspective, but for the sake of Jesus' prayer being realized, can we lay aside our differences of opinion and work together? The benefit of doing so should be obvious. Pooled resources and coordinated efforts will get us farther down the road to accomplishing our goal than duplicated efforts and double expenditures. Logistical problems may not be easy to overcome. Long standing traditions may have to be modified. But our willingness (or unwillingness) to lay aside our opinions and traditions for the sake of unity says a lot about our priorities and our goals.

Jesus knew that the *missio Dei* would benefit from his followers sharing in the oneness he enjoyed with the Father. He also knew his followers would benefit from sharing that oneness.

I will close this section with a quote from Scripture. The point is obvious and needs no further comment. *"The LORD said, 'If as one people speaking the same language they have begun to do this, then nothing they plan to do will be impossible for them'"* (Gen. 11:6 NIV).

Personal and Professional Growth

If you are intellectually, emotionally and spiritually healthy you will continue to study, grow and change throughout your entire life. I have encountered people who were proud of the fact that they had not changed their minds on any important issue in twenty, thirty or forty years. They did not realize that they should be deeply ashamed and embarrassed to admit such a thing. If we are thinking and studying we are growing and changing. Some of the most dramatic spiritual growth a Christian can experience will occur on the mission field, as you experience life from a new

174

perspective, seeing the world through the eyes of a people who have a worldview quite different from your own.

Much of the growth you will experience on the mission field will simply happen. But to take full advantage of your situation and be responsible before God by letting him assist you in reaching your full potential, you need to be engaged in academic pursuits. There are a number of ways you can be engaged in the academic process while in the mission field.

Extension Courses

Language learning will likely fill your days for the first year or so that you are on the field. But once you no longer need to spend nearly full-time in language learning, you should look for ways to continue your education in Bible or missions. Extension courses provide an excellent opportunity. There are a number of fully accredited schools in America and Western Europe that offer extension courses (undergraduate or graduate) that would benefit any missionary. The specific program that you might find most interesting or helpful, given your situation, needs, and interest, is not as important as the fact that you are involved in some form of on-going academic engagement. You need to be challenged. You need to have some way of processing the experiences of your circumstances in the field so you can use your experience to its fullest advantage. Taking an extension course is one way to do this.

Local Colleges and Universities

Local colleges and universities provide an excellent opportunity for missionaries to continue their training. Many missionaries have been able to complete graduate degrees (even Ph.D.s) in local universities. In addition to providing opportunities for additional training, local schools provide additional opportunities for contact with local people, with professors and fellow students alike.

Missiological Journals

If it is simply not possible, or not financially feasible, to take extension courses or attend a local college while in the field, you can still be engaged and stay current with ongoing missiological thinking by receiving missiological journals. Overseas subscriptions may cost a few dollars extra, but the value of having those journals available in the field far exceeds the added expense. There are at least three that, in my opinion, you should receive: *Missiology*, *The International Bulletin of Missionary Research* (IBMR), and *Evangelical Missions Quarterly* (EMQ). These three quarterly journals will provide you with a wide variety of practical and scholarly material to engage and challenge your thinking, and keep you current with what is going on in the study and practice of missions.

Seminars and Continuing Education
While on Furlough

If you cannot manage continuing education while in the field, there are seminars and intensive mission courses you can take while you are home on furlough. Schools offering courses in missions studies often schedule summer "intensives" on a wide range of subjects that may be completed in one or two weeks. A number of mission agencies also schedule mission seminars throughout the year specifically designed for missionaries home on furlough.

Many of the summer intensives offered at schools of mission, or missions seminars offered through the various mission agencies will be advertised in the mission journals. They are held in various parts of the country at different times

176

of the year. Information about dates and locations, topics and speakers may also be available on the internet. If you stay connected to the larger missiological community you will know when and where the seminars and intensives are offered.

Missiological Associations and Societies

Another important source of connection to the larger missiological community is the missiological associations and societies in which you can participate. The *American Missiological Society* is an example of one such association. Missionaries and missions professors from a wide range of religious traditions participate in reading papers, leading and participating in discussions of interest to missionaries, and enjoying fellowship with each other for several days at their annual meeting. There are a number of similar organizations, some larger, some smaller, which offer similar advantages for members. If you are in the field you will not be able to attend each annual meeting, but you can take advantage of the meetings that are scheduled when you are home on furlough.

The main value of membership in a mission association is the additional relationships you will enjoy with missionaries from other parts of the world. Three or four days, meeting with old friends, making new friends, discussing issues that are important to you and to mission endeavors in general can be stimulating and enjoyable, and possibly provide some insight as to how to be more effective in your field work.

Summary

In this brief chapter I have suggested that the missionary is part of a global mission community. In that regard, we need to remember the importance of unity and cooperation in mission endeavors. The Lord's church is larger than any one religious fellowship or tradition. Jesus prayed that the kind of oneness that characterized the relationship he enjoyed with the Father would also characterize the relationship his followers would enjoy with him, with the Father and with each other. Generally speaking, the first 2000 years of our history has not been characterized by the kind of unity among believers Jesus hoped for. Whether or not his prayer is answered depends on our willingness to submit to God's desire for unity. Shall we honor Jesus' prayer for unity?

Not only did Paul condemn division in the Lord's church, he suggested a way of thinking that can be used as a formula for unity. In Ephesians 4:1-6 he said we should be humble and gentle, patient and tolerant, and united in the Holy Spirit. Further, he demonstrated that unity in the body is the natural state of things since the essence of Christianity is oneness: one body, one Spirit, one calling, on Lord, one faith, one baptism, one God.

His metaphor of the church being the body of Christ (1 Cor. 12) teaches us that there is diversity in unity. Unity does not mean uniformity. But unity does mean that we agree on the basics and that we are able to work together in cooperation to participate with God in accomplishing his purpose in the world. We should be able to overcome the logistical problems created by different theological traditions and work together as we serve our Lord.

Another aspect of being part of the global mission community is the need for personal and professional growth so we can participate and contribute in a meaningful way to that community. When we stop studying, thinking, growing, and changing we begin to stagnate. At that point, how effective can we be in our service to the Lord?

To keep from stagnating, missionaries need to be intellectually engaged and challenged. There are a number of ways missionaries can remain engaged and challenged: taking extension courses, reading missiological journals, attending seminars and continuing education courses while on furlough, and participating in missiological associations and societies.

In the next chapter I will discuss books the missionary needs to have in his or her library.

Chapter 8

Building a Missiological Library

In this chapter I will offer some suggestions on important missiological texts missionaries should have in their libraries. If you cannot attend classes at a school that offers missiological studies, the next best thing is to buy and read the books you would read if you were taking classes in missiology.

I will present the authors and their work in alphabetical order, beginning with a complete bibliographical entry, followed by a brief description of the books and its importance to the field of missiology.

Ten Books Missionaries Need to Have

Bosch, David J.
1991   *Transforming Mission: Paradigm Shifts In Theology Of Mission*. Maryknoll: Orbis.

Bosch's *Transforming Mission* is, in my estimation, one of the two most important missiological texts written since Roland Allen's landmark work of 1912, *Missionary Methods: St. Paul's or Ours*. Bosch begins with a brief discussion of the current crisis in mission, which is related to defining "mission" and its place in the theology and life of the church. His thesis is that "it is neither possible nor proper to attempt a revised definition of mission without talking a thorough look at the vicissitudes of missions and the missionary idea during the past twenty centuries of Christian church history" (1991:8).

In Part 1 of his study, Bosch discusses the New Testament

as a "missionary document," paying special attention to Matthew's focus on "disciple-making," Luke's focus on "forgiveness and solidarity with the poor," and Paul's "invitation to join the eschatological community." Part 2 is a historical overview of the church's views and mission methodology over the centuries. In Part 3, Bosch discusses mission in our postmodern era and suggests a number of ways to think about and approach the task of missions.

Bosch's book is a thorough biblical and historical analysis of Christian missions: where we began, where we have been, where we are now, and where we need to go. It provides an essential framework for understanding the many issues that are part of the ongoing process of action, reflection, and action that keeps mission alive and relevant in our ever-changing cultural contexts.

Hiebert, Paul G.
1985 *Anthropological Insights For Missionaries.*
Grand Rapids: Baker.

As the title suggests, Hiebert's study provides missionaries with information they need to do their job more effectively. The information Hiebert offers grows not only out of his own personal experience as a long-term missionary in India, but as an anthropologist as well. He observes that "the modern mission movement was born during a time of Western colonial and technological expansion, and too often Western missionaries equated the gospel with Western civilization. . . . [T]he identification of the gospel with Western power and technology made it foreign, and therefore unacceptable, to many people" (1985:9).

Having begun with that point, Hiebert goes on to discuss the contribution anthropology has made to effective cross-cultural missions, noting that the gospel must function within the framework of human culture. What is the relationship between the gospel and culture? How is one affected by the other? As missionaries take the gospel to other cultures, how are they affected? What must they hold on to, and what must they be willing to release? What is involved in effective cross-cultural ministry?

Hiebert deals with what it means to be an "incarnational missionary," and how missionaries are products (more than they realize) of their Western worldview assumptions. How do those assumptions impact the way missionaries relate to and work with people of other cultures? How do those cultural differences effect the proclamation of the gospel? And how can missionaries assist local people in analyzing their culture in light of God's word, developing a contextualized theology that will be relevant in their contemporary social context?

Hiebert deals with all of these questions (and more), providing missionaries with insights that will improve their effectiveness as ambassadors of Christ.

Hiebert, Paul G., R. Daniel Shaw, and Tite Tienou.
1999 *Understanding Folk Religion: A Christian Response to Popular Beliefs and Practices.* **Grand Rapids: Baker.**

In explaining why they wrote the book, Hiebert, Shaw, and Tienou say that "it became increasingly clear that missionaries must not only study Scripture and the formal religions of the people they serve, but also the day-to-day religious beliefs and practices that rule the people's lives if they wanted to communicate the gospel as an answer to all the people's hopes and fears" (1999:9). Their purpose for writing is to "sensitize Christians to the need to deal with folk religions, and to understand them."

What is folk religion? The authors explain what folk

religion is, illustrating what they mean by discussing various elements of folk religions throughout the world. In the simplest terms, folk religion is the way religion is understood and practiced by the people, which may be different (in some cases substantially different) than the official explanation of belief and practice given by religious leaders. Hiebert, Shaw, and Tienou explain how missionaries can respond to folk religions in the proclamation of the gospel and the development of contextualized Christian theologies. Their work is divided into four sections: 1) developing an analytical model, 2) folk religious beliefs, 3) folk religious practices, and 4) Christian responses to folk religion.

This is an important work because what missionaries encounter in the field while working with people is often not what they expect to encounter based on what they learned or read about concerning the formal religious beliefs of those people. Hiebert, Shaw, and Tienou help missionaries to respond to those unexpected things that come up when carrying the gospel across cultural boundaries.

Kraft, Charles H.
   1979   *Christianity in Culture: A Study in Dynamic Biblical Theologizing in Cross-Cultural Perspective.* Maryknoll: Orbis.

In discussing Bosch' book, *Transforming Mission,* I said that in my estimation it was one of the two most significant missiological texts of our day. Kraft's *Christianity in Culture* is the other one. Kraft raises questions that may make readers uncomfortable. He may reach conclusion with which readers find it difficult to agree. But regardless of one's level of comfort or agreement, Kraft will make readers think. The observations he makes and the questions he raises are legitimate, and dealing with them is absolutely essential if we are to be effective cross-cultural witnesses.

One of the many significant issues Kraft addresses has to do with the way we perceive reality. Everyone tends to think that the way they see and understand the world is the correct and sensible (and only) way to see and understand the world. What we fail to realize is that our perception of reality is based on our limited and culturally influenced perspective.

In Part 1 of his book, Kraft not only reminds us of our culturally influenced and limited perception of reality, he suggests a biblical model for perceiving the world around us. In Part 2, Kraft discusses the cultural matrix, including worldview, cultural forms, patterns, and processes, and discusses how to evaluate cultural forms.

In Part 3, Kraft discusses how God relates to culture. Is God against culture, in culture, or above culture? Kraft concludes that God is above culture but works in and through culture to accomplish his purposes. In Part 4, Kraft discusses God's revelation to humans, suggesting a biblical way to understand the nature of Scripture.

In Part 5, the discussion has to do with the content of the gospel: the content does not change, but the presentation must. This is Kraft's discussion of *Dynamic Equivalence* in translation, in the *transculturation* of the message, and in the process of theologizing. In the final section, Part 6, Kraft discusses how a contextualized form of the one gospel may affect the forms and structures associated with it, that is, with the way worship and Christian living are accomplished.

Even if missionaries end up disagreeing with Kraft's conclusions, his discussion of the issues and problems is a must read for everyone who wants to be a cross-cultural witness for Christ. The questions Kraft raises must be addressed. Those who do not agree with his proposed solutions are free to develop their own.

Kraft, Charles H.
1996 *Anthropology For Christian Witness.* **Maryknoll:**
Orbis.

Another significant and useful book by Kraft is his cultural anthropology text. A thorough anthropology text written from a Christian point of view is hard to find. Kraft has provided believers with a fine example of scholarship and faith, demonstrating that anthropology and Christianity are not mutually exclusive. Far from it. Anthropology can be a powerful tool in the hands of a knowledgeable believer.

Kraft begins by discussing the ways in which anthropology commends itself to the missiological task, discussing ten ways anthropology is useful in cross-cultural witnessing. Topics he discusses in Part 1 include: how humans perceive reality, what culture is, worldview, how to think cross-culturally, God's role in culture, and human beings and race. In Part 2, he discusses culture in more detail, including a model of culture, the role of forms and meaning in culture, and how individuals are impacted by their culture. Part 3 is a discussion of the many ways humans relate to the universe, while Part 4 focuses on how we relate to other people, including discussions of communication, education, family, status and role, groupings, and social control. In Part 5, Kraft discusses culture and worldview change, leading the reader through the maze of issues related to cross-cultural ministry and the changes (including changes in worldview) that must accompany Christian conversion. In his final section, Part 6, Kraft speaks to the need for further research and study in the field of anthropology.

Kraft's approach to anthropology is thoroughly Christian. Each chapter begins with an integration thought, bridging what he discusses in that chapter with the ideas and principles communicated in Scripture. A thorough familiarity with the information in *Anthropology For Christian Witness* will help missionaries do a better job of cross-cultural witnessing.

Moreau, A. Scott, Editor
2000 *Evangelical Dictionary of World Missions.* **Grand Rapids: Baker.**

This dictionary contains over 1,400 articles on the theory, practice, theology, and history of missions from over 300 missionaries, theologians and educators representing a wide range of theological traditions and cultural backgrounds. The articles are thorough, scholarly, and up-to-date. It is an essential tool in the library of a missiologist.

Muller, Karl, Theo Sundermeier, Stephen B. Bevans, and Richard H. Bliese, Editors
1998 *Dictionary of Mission: Theology, History, Perspectives.* **Maryknoll: Orbis.**

This dictionary, though not as exhaustive as the *Evangelical Dictionary* mentioned above, is also an excellent resource for missions studies. A different group of missions scholars approach many of the same topics from a slightly different point of view allowing these two volumes to become complimentary voices on important missiological topics of study. Having access to both of them provides missionaries with more than one point of view in their studies.

Peters, George W.
1972 *A Biblical Theology of Missions.* **Chicago: Moody.**

Though Peters' work is older, its quality assures its continued use. Peters breaks his eight chapters into three sections: the biblical foundations of missions, the biblical delineation of missions, and the biblical instruments and dynamics of missions. It is thoroughly rooted in the biblical text, allowing Scripture to guide the discussion. For Peters, mission grows out of the nature of God and his purpose in the world. Mission is rooted in Jesus, flowing from the Old Testament, where it is introduced, into the New, where it receives its fullest expression in the sacrifice of Jesus and the sending of the church into all the world.

Peters is thorough yet concise, unifying and integrating a wide range of theological themes without overwhelming the reader. He manages to demonstrate that a biblical theology is also a mission theology, for God's mission in the world is to save the lost.

Winter, Ralph D. and Steven C. Hawthorne, Editors
    1999 *Perspectives on the World Christian Movement.*
    Pasadena: William Carey.

While this work is not technically a dictionary or an encyclopedia, it is a collection of 124 articles on various aspects of missions by some of the leading missiologists of the late twentieth century. Its four major sections, the biblical perspective, the historical perspective, the cultural perspective, and the strategic perspective, make it an important text for anyone studying missions. *Perspectives* provides the reader with some of the best thinking God's people have done on the subject of missions.

Van Engen, Charles
    1996 *Mission on the Way: Issues in Mission Theology.*
    Grand Rapids: Baker.

What theological presuppositions underlie the practice of

missions? The answer to that question would depend on who was being asked. In this book, Van Engen answers that question by discussing the relationship between mission theology and the Bible, focusing on the importance of narrative theology, which highlights the "story" told in Scripture rather than history, doctrine or law. Van Engen also discusses the role of context in mission theology, paying special attention to the challenges of constructing contextual theologies in an urban setting.

Chapter six marks a shift in direction (over several chapters) as Van Engen highlights the history of missions up to contemporary times, including a discussion of the impact postmodern thinking has had on missions. His closing chapters focus on mission theology and ministry formation, discussing the role of the minister as a missionary leader and the changes he believes are necessary for adequate training of mission personnel today.

Van Engen's title, *Mission on the Way*, suggests that mission theology is an ongoing process. Reflection about how we do missions happens as we are in the process of participating with God in his purpose for the world. Missions and mission theology happen as we go . . . *on the way*. Van Engen reminds us of that while prompting us to greater action-reflection-action.

Summary

My purpose in this chapter has been to create a basic reading list for students of missions. The books I have listed are foundational, and in no way constitute a complete missiological reading list. Such a list would easily include several hundred books. The volumes I have recommended cover the basics of missiological studies as divided into the threefold sections of Word, World, and Church.

My recommendation for missiological studies is to enroll in a college or seminary that offers missions studies. However, if one cannot do that, reading missiological texts is the next best thing. These ten books are enough to get you started. Beyond these, the "References Cited" section of this book will give you a wide range of other options for readings in missions. An additional bibliography of books specifically related to anthropology and contextualization that are not part of this list can be found in Appendix A.

Conclusion

God created human beings in his image so he and they could enjoy a mutually satisfying relationship with each other. When human sin ruined the relationship, God set out to solve the problem, making it possible for his estranged human children to be reconciled to him, so the kind of relationship he had originally envisioned could be a reality once again. God's interaction in human history, including 1) his selection and calling of Abraham, 2) his establishing the nation of Israel, 3) the Sinaitic Covenant, 4) his ongoing (and often strained) relationship with the people of Israel, 5) his incarnation, 6) the ministry, death, and resurrection of Jesus, and 7) the sending of Jesus' disciples into the world to tell the story of God's desire for a relationship with all people, and of his grace and mercy which make the relationship possible, were all part of the *missio Dei*, God's mission in the world.

As God's people, Christians participate with him in his mission in the world. The church's "mission" is to work with God in accomplishing his mission. Missiology is the study of how God's people participate with him as he works to accomplish his mission in the world. Missiology is a multidisciplinary discipline, involving theological, anthropological and ecclesiological studies, otherwise referred to as Word, World and Church. God's Word tells the story of his desire for a relationship with all people, providing the impetus for missions. It also tells us how the early church, following the leadership of the Holy Spirit, participated with God in accomplishing his mission in the world. It tells us what we should do, why we should do it and provides us with an example of how early believers told the story of Jesus throughout the Roman world.

The church today needs to remember that missions is the primary purpose of the church. Believers need to open

191

themselves to the Spirit's prompting, discovering how he wants to use them in accomplishing God's purpose in the world today. There are many ways to participate with God in his mission in the world. One does not have to be a trained theologian in order to be involved in missions. Doctors, nurses, accountants, mechanics, carpenters, plumbers, dentists, electricians, computer programmers, teachers, writers, airplane pilots, radio announcers, translators, general maintenance people, counselors, secretaries, and a host of other specialists are needed in missions efforts around the world.

Missions is not just for young people. In fact, in many cultures, more mature people (especially those with gray hair) will be granted a higher status and have an advantage in foreign cultures that younger missionaries will not enjoy for many years. This means that mature people who have enjoyed successful careers in fields other than theology, after acquiring the cross-cultural training they need, can be valuable participants in God's mission.

Missions is not always in far away remote places. Missions can be down the street around the corner. Wherever it is, current trends in population shifts mean that it will likely be done in an urban setting. Metropolises and megacities are growing at a phenomenal rate. By the year 2025, the majority of the world's population will live in cities. Missions in cities will involve many challenges. Poverty, crime, addiction, abuse, homelessness, and a host of other issues will have to be addressed by God's people if we are to make a difference in the lives of those who need to be reconciled to God.

Life as a missionary can be difficult. The loss of familiar cultural landmarks (culture shock) can be debilitating, especially for those not adequately prepared for what they will encounter. Sometimes the hardest part of being a missionary is getting along with other missionaries. Spiritual maturity and continued growth is essential for success. Missionaries must continue to study and grow as Christians and as missionaries. They must be academically engaged so that they are stretched and challenged as they participate in the larger missionary community. If missionaries cannot stay academically engaged by participating in an on-line or distance a learning program while in the field, they can at least read missiological texts while in the field and participate in missions seminars when home on furlough.

Early believers told the story of Jesus, sharing their faith with others everywhere they went. The church today needs to refocus on the importance of telling the story of Jesus. It is a story that begins and ends with God's desire for a relationship with all people.

Appendix A

Books on anthropology and contextualization

Bevans, Stephen
1992 *Models of Contextual Theology*. Maryknoll: Obris.

Dyrness, William A.
1990 *Learning About Theology From The Third World*. Grand Rapids: Zondervan.

1992 *Invitation To Cross-Cultural Awareness: Case Studies In Vernacular Theologies*. Grand Rapids: Zondervan.

Hiebert, Paul G.
1994 *Anthropological Reflections on Missiological Issues*. Grand Rapids: Baker.

Lingenfelter, Sherwood
1996 *Agents Of Transformation: A Guide For Effective Cross-Cultural Ministry*. Grand Rapids: Baker.

1998 *Transforming Culture: A Challenge For Christian Mission*. Grand Rapids:Baker.

Loewen, Jacob A.
1975 *Culture And Human Values: Christian Intervention In Anthropological Perspective*. Pasadena: William Carey.

2000 *The Bible In Cross-Cultural Perspective*. Pasadena: William Carey.

Luzbetak, Louis J.
1988 *The Church And Cultures: New Perspectives In Missiological Anthropology*. Maryknoll: Orbis.

Schreiter, Robert J.
1985 *Constructing Local Theologies*. Maryknoll: Orbis.

Works Cited

Action For Orphans
    2000   FactSheet: Children Orphaned By AIDS: A
    Global Perspective January, 2000. Accessed January 25,
    2002 <http://orphans.fxb.org/inform/reports.html>

Anderson, B. W.
    1962   "Creation," in *The Interpreter's Dictionary of the
    Bible*. George Buttrick, ed. Nashville: Abingdon.

Anderson, Ray S.
    1986 *On Being Human: Essays in Theological
    Anthropology*. Pasadena: Fuller Seminary Press.

Barnett Betty
    1991   *Friend Raising: Building A Missionary Support
    Team That Lasts*. Seattle: YWAM.

Barrett, David B, and Todd M. Johnson
    2002   "Annual Statistical Table on Global Mission:
    2002. *International Bulletin of Missionary Research* 26
    (1) 22-23.

Bevans, Stephen B.
    1992   *Models Of Contextual Theology. Maryknoll*:
    Orbis.

Bosch, David J.
    1991   *Transforming Mission: Paradigm Shifts In
    Theology Of Mission*. Maryknoll: Orbis.

Brewster, Elizabeth S. and E. Thomas Brewster
    1976   *Language Acquisition Made Practical: Field
    Methods for Language Learners*. Pasadena: Lungua
    House.

Brierley, Peter W.
1997 "Missionary Attrition: The ReMAP Research Project," in *Too Valuable to Lose: Exploring the Causes and Cures of Missionary Attrition*. William D. Taylor, ed. Pasadena: William Carey.

Bromiley, Geoffrey W.
1978 *Historical Theology: An Introduction*. Grand Rapids: Eerdmans.

Brueggemann, Walter
1982 *Genesis Interpretation: A Bible Commentary for Preaching and Teaching*. Atlanta: John Knox.

Campbell, Evvy
2000 "Medical Mission Work," in *Evangelical Dictionary Of World Missions*. A Scott Moreau, ed. Grand Rapids: Baker.

Chadwick, Henry
1993 *The Early Church: The Story of Emergent Christianity From the Apostolic Age To The Dividing Of The Ways Between The Greek East And The Latin West*. London: Penguin.

Childs, Brevard S.
1992 *Biblical Theology of the Old and New Testaments: Theological Reflection On The Christian Bible*. Minneapolis: Fortress.

Clinton, Robert J.
1989 *Leadership Emergence Theory*. Altadena: Barnabas.

Coote, Robert T.
    1995 "Good News, Bad News: North American Protestant Overseas Personnel Statistics In Twenty-five Year Perspective" *International Bulletin Of Missionary Research.* 19 (1) 6-13.

Culture Grams
    2001 *Culture Grams: People, The World, You.* Accessed February 1, 2002
    http://www.culturegrams.com

Demarest, Bruce A.
    1984 "Systematic Theology," in *Evangelical Dictionary Of Theology.* Walter Elwell, ed. Grand Rapids: Baker.

Dillion, William P.
    1993 *People Raising: A Practical Guide To Raising Support.* Chicago: Moody.

Donovan, Kath and Ruth Myors
    1997 "Reflections On Attrition In Career Missionaries: A Generational Perspective Into The Future," in *Too Valuable To Lose: Exploring The Causes And Cures Of Missionary Attrition.* William D. Taylor, ed. Pasadena: William Carey.

Dowley, Tim
    1995 *Introduction To The History of Christianity.* Tim Dowley, ed. Minneapolis: Fortress.

Dyrness, William A.
    1990 *Learning About Theology From The Third World.* Grand Rapids: Zondervan.

    1992 *Invitation To Cross-Cultural Awareness: Case Studies In Vernacular Theologies.* Grand Rapids: Zondervan.

Ekstrom, Bertil
    1997 "The Selection Process And The Issue Of
    Attrition: Perspective Of The New Sending Countries,"
    in *Too Valuable To Lose: Exploring The Causes And
    Cures Of Missionary Attrition*. William Taylor, ed.
    Pasadena: William Carey.

Ember, Melvin and Carol Ember
    2000 *Countries And Their Cultures*. Melvin Ember
    and Carol Ember, eds. New York: Macmillan.

Enns, Paul
    1989 *The Moody Handbook Of Theology*. Chicago:
    Moody.

George, Timothy
    1991 *Faithful Witness: The Life And Mission Of
    William Carey*. Birmingham: New Hope.

Gilliland, Dean
    2000 "Contextualization," in *Evangelical Dictionary of
    World Missions*. A. Scott Moreau, ed. Grand Rapids:
    Baker.

Giron, Rodolfo
    1997 "An Integrated Model Of Missions." In *Too
    Valuable To Lose: Exploring The Causes And Cures Of
    Missionary Attrition*. William Taylor, ed. Pasadena:
    William Carey.

Glick, Thomas F.
    1997 "Acculturation," in *The Dictionary of
    Anthropology*. Thomas Barfield, ed. Malden: Blackwell.

Goldingay, John
    1998 "On Being Human," in *Theology News and
    Notes*. December.

Grunlan, Stephan A. and Marvin K. Mayers
1988   *Cultural Anthropology: A Christian Perspective.*
Grand Rapids: Zondervan.

Hamilton, Victor P.
1990   *The Book of Genesis.* Grand Rapids: Eerdmans.

Hesselgrave, David J.
1991   *Communicating Christ Cross-Culturally: An Introduction To Missionary Communication.* Grand Rapids: Zondervan.

1980   *Planting Churches Cross-Culturally: A Guide For Home And Foreign Missions.* Grand Rapids: Baker.

Hiebert, Paul G.
1985   *Anthropological Insights For Missionaries.* Grand Rapids: Baker.

1983   *Cultural Anthropology.* Grand Rapids: Baker.

1994   *Anthropological Reflections On Missiological Issues.* Grand Rapids: Baker.

Hinson, E. Glenn
1996   *The Early Church: Origins To The Dawn Of The Middle Ages.* Nashville: Abingdon.

Johnstone, Patrick and Jason Mandryk
2001   *Operation World: 21ˢᵗ Century Edition.* Harrisonburg: Bethany.

Kaiser, Walter C.
2000   *Mission In The Old Testament: Israel As A Light To The Nations.* Grand Rapids: Baker.

Kidner, Derek
1967 *Genesis: An Introduction and Commentary.*
Downers Grove: InterVarsity Press.

Kirk, Andrew J.
2000 *What Is Mission: Theological Explorations.*
Minneapolis: Fortress.

Kraft, Charles H.
1979 *Christianity In Culture: A Study In Dynamic Biblical Theologizing In Cross-Cultural Perspective.*
Maryknoll: Orbis.

1996 *Anthropology For Christian Witness.* Maryknoll: Orbis.

2000 *"Worldview And Worldview Change,"* MB 525 Class Syllabus. Pasadena: Fuller Theological Seminary School of World Mission.

2000 b "Culture Shock," in *Evangelical Dictionary of world Missions.* A. Scott Moreau, ed. Grand Rapids: Baker.

Latourette, Kenneth Scott
1975 *A History of Christianity: Volume I Beginnings To 1500.* San Francisco: Harper.

Lingenfelter, Sherwood
1996 *Agents Of Transformation: A Guide For Effective Cross-Cultural Ministry.* Grand Rapids: Baker.

1998 *Transforming Culture: A Challenge For Christian Mission.* Grand Rapids: Baker.

Lingenfelter, Judith
2001 "Training Future Leaders In Our Classrooms,"
Missiology. XXIX (4) 449-459.

Lingerfelter, Sherwood and Marvin Mayers
1986 *Ministering Cross-Culturally: An Incarnational
Model For Personal Relationships.* Grand Rapids:
Baker.

Loewen, Jacob A.
1975 *Culture And Human Values: Christian
Intervention In Anthropological Perspective.* Pasadena:
William Carey.

2000 *The Bible In Cross-Cultural Perspective.*
Pasadena: William Carey.

Longnecker, Richard N.
1975 *Biblical Exegesis In The Apostolic Period.* Grand
Rapids: Eerdmans.

Love, Richard
2000 "10/40 Window," in *Evangelical Dictionary Of
World Missions.* A. Scott Moreau, ed. Grand Rapids:
Baker.

Lyons, Enda
1994 *Jesus: Self-Portrait By God.* New York: Paulist.

Luzbeak, Louis J.
1988 *The Church And Cultures: New Perspectives In
Missiological Anthropology.* Maryknoll: Orbis.

Markus, Robert A
2001 "From Rome To The Barbarian Kingdoms (330-
700)," in *The Oxford Illustrated History Of Christianity.*
John McManners, ed. Oxford: Oxford University Press.

Mathews, Kenneth A.
1996 *The New American Commentary: An Exegetical and Theological Exposition of Holy Scripture Genesis 1-11:26*. Nashville: Broadman & Holman.

McGrath, Alister, E.
1997 *Christian Theology: An Introduction*. Oxford: Blackwell.

McIntosh, John A.
2000 "Missio Dei," in *Evangelical Dictionary Of world Missions*. A. Scott Moreau, ed. Grand Rapids: Baker.

Mission Aviation Fellowship
2002 *Who We Are*. Accessed January 25, 2002. <http://www.maf.org/MAF.asp?Category=About&Document=About>

Moreau, A. Scott
2000 "Mission And Missions," in *Evangelical Dictionary Of World Missions*. A. Scott Moreau, ed. Grand Rapids: Baker.

Muller, Karl, et.al.
1998 *Dictionary of Mission: Theology, History, Perspective*. Karl Muller, ed. Maryknoll: Orbis.

National Center On Addiction And Substance Abuse At Columbia University
1996 *Spirituality And Religion Reduce Risk Of Substance Abuse*. Accessed January 25, 2002 <http://www.casacolumbia.org/newsletter1457/newsletter_show.htm?doc_id=91374>

National Clearinghouse On Child Abuse And Neglect
Information
    1996   Executive Summary Of The Third National
    Incident Study Of Child Abuse And Neglect. Accessed
    January 25, 2002
    <http://www.calib.com/nccanch/pubs/statinfo/nis3.cfm>

National Coalition For The Homeless
    1999   NCH Fact Sheet #2: How Many People
    Experience Homelessness? Accessed January 25, 2002
    <http://nch.ari.net/numbers.html>

Neely, Alan
    2000   "Missiology," in *Evangelical Dictionary Of
    World Missions*. A. Scott Moreau, ed. Grand Rapids:
    Baker.

Neill, Stephen
    1990   *A History Of Christian Missions*. London:
    Penguin.

Newbigin, Leslie
    1986   *Foolishness To The Greeks: The Gospel And
    Western Culture*. Grand Rapids: Eerdmans.

Nida, Eugene A. and William D. Reyburn
    1981   *Meaning Across Culture*. Maryknoll: Orbis.

Ott, Craig
    2001   "Matching The Church Planter's Role With The
    Church Planting Model." *Evangelical Missions
    Quarterly*. 37 (3) 338-344.

Pearson, Paul E.
    1998   *Historical Development Of The Christian
    Movement*. MH520 Class Syllabus. Pasadena, CA:
    Fuller Theological Seminary School of World Mission.

Peters, George W.
1972 *A Biblical Theology Of Missions*. Chicago:
Moody.

Porter, J. R.
1993 "Creation," in *The Oxford Companion To The
Bible*. Bruce Metzger and Michael Coogan, eds. New
York: Oxford University Press.

Reventlow, Henning Graf
1992 "Theology (Biblical), History Of," in *The Anchor
Bible Dictionary*. David Noel Freedman, ed. New York:
Doubleday.

Rogers, Everett M.
1995 *Diffusion Of Innovations*. New York: The Free
Press.

Rogers, Glenn
2002 *God's Desire For A Relationship With All
People: The Metatheme Of Scripture*. Ph.D. dissertation
Fuller Theological Seminary.

Rosner, Brian S.
2000 "Biblical Theology," in *New Dictionary Of
Biblical Theology*. T. Desmond Alexander and Brian S.
Rosner, eds. Downers Grove: Inter-Varsity.

Saal, William J.
1991 *Reaching Muslims For Christ*. Chicago: Moody.

Schreiter, Robert J.
1985 *Constructing Local Theologies*. Maryknoll:
Orbis.

Shaw, R. Daniel and Charles Van Engen
1998 *Proclaiming God's Word In Today's World:
God's Truth or Hocus Pocus*. Unpublished Manuscript.

Shaw, R. Daniel
    1988   Transculturation: The Cultural Factor in
    Translation and Other Communication Tasks. Pasadena:
    William Carey.

    1990   *Kandila: Samo Ceremonialism And Interpersonal
    Relationships*. Ann Arbor: University of Michigan
    Press.

    2000   "Bible Translation," in *Evangelical Dictionary Of
    World Missions*. A. Scott Moreau, ed. Grand Rapids:
    Baker.

Shink, Wilbert R.
    2001   "Recasting Theology Of Mission: Impulses From
    The Non-Western World" *International Bulletin Of
    Missionary Research* 25 (3) 98-107.

Snow, Donald B.
    2001   *English Teaching As Christian Mission: An
    Applied Theology*. Scottdale: Herald.

Stamoolis, James
    2001   "How Are We Doing At Developing National
    Leaders?" *Evangelical Missions Quarterly*. 37 (4) 488-
    495.

Stuart, Douglas
    1992   "Exegesis," in *The Anchor Bible Dictionary*.
    David Noel Freedman, ed. New York: Doubleday.

Thiselton, Anthony C.
    1993   "Hermeneutics," in *The Oxford Companion To
    The Bible*. Bruce Metzger, Michael Coogan, eds. New
    York: Oxford.

United Nations Office For Drug Control And Crime
Prevention. *2001 World Drug Report.*
    Accesses January 25, 2002.
    <http://www.odccp.org/world_drug_report.html>

Van Engen, Charles
    1996 *Mission On The Way: Issues In Mission
    Theology.* Grand Rapids: Baker.

    2000 "Theology Of Mission," in *Evangelical
    Dictionary Of World Missions.* A. Scott Moreau, ed.
    Grand Rapids: Baker.

Van Rheenen, Gailyn
    1996 *Missions: Biblical Foundations And
    Contemporary Strategies.* Grand Rapids: Zondervan.

Verkuyl, Johannes
    1978 *Contemporary Mission: An Introduction.* Grand
    Rapids: Eerdmans.

Von Rad, Gerhard
    1961 *Genesis: A Commentary.* Philadelphia:
    Westminster.

Wenham, Gordon J.
    1987 *Word Biblical Commentary: Genesis 1-15.*
    Waco: Word.

Willis, John T.
    1979 *The Living Word Commentary: Genesis.* Austin:
    Sweet.

Woman's Coalition Of St. Croix
    2002 *Domestic Violence: Facts About Domestic
    Violence.* Accessed January 25, 2002.
    <http://www.wcstx.com/domsticv.htm>

Printed in the United States
88470LV00006B/298-303/A